OODLES *of* NOODLES

from the Home Library Test Kitchen

Cole's Home Library Cookbooks
Glen Ellen, California

Cole's **Home** **Library** cookbooks

OODLES *of* NOODLES

Gingery fried bean-curd pouches with wasabi, page 18

Contents

4
Miso, laksa & other great soups

In Asia, soup is often served as a main course, or to signal the end of a meal. But no matter when it appears, a noodle-rich soup is always in order

16
Just for starters

First course, finger food or light meal, this lovely selection of imaginatively appetising dishes guarantees that the occasion starts off with a bang

30
Prime-time salads

No longer relegated to the dinner table's sidelines, these noodle-bedecked salads legitimately command a peak-viewing timeslot on your menu

42
Meat with the works

Meat enjoys such a happy affinity with the noodle that there's no end to the number of ways they can marry in the kitchen... share in the celebration

⊏ **A picture is worth a thousand words...** Noodle packaging information can sometimes be misleading or even incorrectly translated so it's important that you can actually identify what's inside the package, regardless of what name the manufacturer has given it. To help, we've included a sample of each noodle, before it was cooked, in the same picture as the finished dish in which it's used.

Lime-roasted game hen with noodles, page 66

Vietnamese beef noodle soup, page 10

Noodles, by any other name...

Don't worry if you can't find exactly the same noodle we call for: as long as you use one made from the same basic ingredient (wheat flour, rice flour, etc), go for fresh or dried as we've done, and adjust cooking times and methods accordingly, you're bound to achieve perfectly satisfactory results.

64
Counting your chickens

Hatch a mealtime plot with this selection of poultry and noodle combos. Fowl-play turns to fare game when such natural partners come home to roost

82
Fishing for compliments

The multitude of fishes we're blessed with in this country is an even match for the numerous noodles available in this delectable cache of sea-treasures

98
Ca'noodling with vegetables

Putting their heads together, veggies and noodles indulge us with irresistible flavours so well-matched that cook and diner alike will coo with delight

Glossary 113
Index 117

For more Cole's Home Library information on noodle cuisine, including cookbooks for the home cook, see page 120 or come to Cole's web site, www.coleshomelibrary.com, for an interactive tour of what is happening in the world of cooking, gardening, and crafts for today's creative lifestyle.

Beef with sun-dried tomato sauce, page 42

Miso, laksa and other great soups

◧ When unexpected guests arrived, our parents used to joke that they'd "just throw another cup of water in the soup." Today, the expression should be amended to "just add noodles" because we've all come to appreciate what a satisfying extender they are. In this recipe selection we've followed the Asian lead to create a line-up of soups, which can be a meal on their own, or part of a larger menu.

COCONUT SPINACH SOUP

Use either somyun, Korean wheat noodles, or somen, the Japanese version, for this recipe.

3 tablespoons vegetable oil
1 medium onion, chopped
2 cloves garlic, crushed
1¹/₂ tablespoons chopped fresh ginger
1¹/₂ tablespoons garam masala
1 teaspoon ground cardamom
1 teaspoon cumin seeds, crushed
1 teaspoon coriander seeds, crushed
2lb spinach, trimmed
2 large potatoes, chopped
2¹/₂ cups chicken stock
1²/₃ cups coconut milk
8oz dried wheat noodles
1 cup cream
3 tablespoons lime juice
¹/₄ cup shredded coconut, toasted

Heat oil in medium pan; cook onion, garlic, ginger, spices and seeds, stirring, until onion is soft. Add spinach and potatoes; stir until spinach is wilted. Stir in stock and coconut milk. Bring to boil; simmer, uncovered, 30 minutes.

Meanwhile, cook noodles in large pan of boiling salted water, uncovered, until just tender; drain. Cover to keep warm.

Blend or process spinach mixture, in batches, until smooth; return to pan. Stir in cream and juice; stir over heat, without boiling, until hot.

Divide noodles among serving bowls, ladle in hot soup; sprinkle with coconut.

SERVES 6 TO 8

Best made just before serving

MEATBALLS IN BROTH WITH GARLIC CROUTONS

Shanghai's cuisine responds to its long, cold winters: robust, nourishing noodles are the daily staple rather than rice in this wheat-growing region.

2 slices whole wheat bread
1 clove garlic, crushed
3 tablespoons vegetable oil
1lb lean ground lamb
2 tablespoons chopped
  fresh sage
5 cloves garlic, crushed, extra
4 cups beef stock
2 cups vegetable stock
1 1/2 tablespoons sugar
2 tablespoons finely chopped
  fresh lemon grass
1 tablespoon finely grated lime rind
10 1/2 oz dried Shanghai noodles
4oz enoki mushrooms
3 green onions, sliced

Discard crusts from bread; cut bread into small dice. Combine garlic and oil in medium bowl; toss bread until coated. Place bread in single layer on oven tray. Bake at 350°F about 10 minutes or until croutons are browned and crisp.

Combine lamb, sage, and 3 cloves of the extra garlic in medium bowl. Roll heaped tablespoons of mixture into balls; place on tray. Cover; refrigerate 1 hour.

Heat stocks in large pan; salt to taste. Add remaining extra garlic, sugar, lemon grass and rind. Bring to boil; simmer, uncovered, 5 minutes. Add meatballs and noodles to the stock mixture. Bring to boil; boil, uncovered, 4 minutes or until meatballs are cooked through. Divide mushrooms and onions among serving bowls. Ladle in hot broth with noodles and meatballs; scatter with croutons.

SERVES 4 TO 6

Meatballs can be prepared 1 day ahead

Storage Covered, in refrigerator
Freeze Uncooked meatballs suitable

◻ **SHANGHAI NOODLES** are made from semolina, the coarsely-milled inner part of durum wheat; they are sold fresh, as a thick, spaghetti-type noodle, or dried, as a thin white noodle. Depending on the recipe, various kinds of fresh or dried wheat noodles could be substituted.

ROASTED TOMATO AND PINTO BEAN SOUP

We used somen, a Japanese wheat noodle, but any thin noodle works well in this soup.

20 large plum tomatoes,
  halved lengthwise
1 teaspoon salt
1 teaspoon cracked black pepper
1/2 large garlic bulb
1 1/2 tablespoons olive oil
1 large onion, chopped
5 cups vegetable stock
1/4 cup loosely packed fresh basil
1 1/2 tablespoons balsamic vinegar
1 teaspoon sugar
14oz can pinto beans,
  rinsed, drained
3 1/2 oz somen
3 tablespoons shredded fresh
  basil, extra

Place tomatoes, cut side up, on wire racks over baking dishes, sprinkle with salt and pepper. Wrap unpeeled garlic bulb in foil, place on rack with tomatoes. Bake, uncovered, at 350°F 1 1/2 hours or until softened; cool. Squeeze garlic from skins; reserve pulp, discard skins.

Heat oil in large pan; cook onion, stirring, until soft. Add tomatoes, garlic pulp, stock, basil, vinegar and sugar. Bring to boil; simmer, covered, 15 minutes.

Blend or process tomato mixture in batches until smooth. Return tomato mixture to pan with beans. Bring to boil, stirring, 2 minutes.

Meanwhile, cook noodles in medium pan of boiling salted water, uncovered, until just tender; drain.

Divide noodles among bowls. Ladle in hot soup; sprinkle with extra basil.

SERVES 6

Best made just before serving

Opposite Meatballs in broth with garlic croutons
Below Roasted tomato and pinto bean soup

THAI PUMPKIN SOUP

We used pumpkin and mung bean thread noodles in this, our version of the traditional Thai favorite, gaeng lieng fak thong.

3 tablespoons peanut oil
3lb pumpkin, chopped
2 medium carrots, chopped
1 large potato, chopped
1 large onion, chopped
6 cups chicken stock
1¹/₂ tablespoons sambal oelek
2 tablespoons finely chopped fresh lemon grass
1¹/₂ tablespoons lime juice
2 teaspoons garam masala
3¹/₂ oz bean thread noodles
1 cup coconut milk
¹/₄ cup shredded coconut, toasted
3 tablespoons fresh cilantro

Heat oil in large pan; cook pumpkin, carrot, potato and onion, stirring, until browned lightly. Stir in stock, sambal oelek, lemon grass, juice and garam masala. Bring to boil; simmer, uncovered, 30 minutes.

Meanwhile, cut noodles into 2-inch lengths, place in medium heatproof bowl, cover with boiling water, let stand until just tender; drain.

Blend or process vegetable mixture, in batches, until smooth; return to pan. Stir in milk and noodles. Bring to boil; simmer, stirring, 2 minutes.

Ladle hot soup into serving bowls; sprinkle with coconut and cilantro.

SERVES 6 TO 8

Best made just before serving

COCONUT CHICKEN SOUP

Tom kha gai is a Thai soup that has made its way into our lives on a regular basis. Try our version, using fresh thin egg noodles.

- **4 cups chicken stock**
- **1³/₄ cups coconut milk**
- **¹/₃ cup lime juice**
- **¹/₄ cup fish sauce**
- **2 tablespoons finely chopped fresh lemon grass**
- **6 kaffir lime leaves, torn**
- **3 fresh cilantro roots**
- **1 teaspoon brown sugar**
- **4 small fresh red chilis, seeded, sliced**
- **2 large boneless chicken breasts, sliced thinly**
- **6oz fresh egg noodles**
- **¹/₃ cup loosely packed fresh cilantro**

Add stock, milk, juice, sauce, lemon grass, lime leaves, coriander roots, sugar and half the chilis to large pan. Bring to boil; simmer, covered, 30 minutes. Discard coriander roots. Bring soup mixture to boil; stir in chicken and noodles. Bring to boil; simmer, covered, 1 minute. Ladle hot soup into serving bowls; sprinkle with cilantro and remaining chili.

SERVES 4

Best made just before serving

⊏ **BEAN THREAD NOODLES** are sometimes known as cellophane or glass noodles because they are transparent when cooked, but are also well-known as bean thread vermicelli. Soak them only until they are soft — any longer and they become stodgy or start to dissolve.

MISO SOUP

There are as many varieties of this clear Japanese soup as there are families in Japan. We used "white" miso (tan in color) and mung bean thread noodles.

- **3¹/₂ oz bean thread noodles**
- **¹/₃ cup miso (soy bean paste)**
- **6 cups water**
- **2¹/₂ teaspoons dashi granules**
- **10¹/₂ oz block firm tofu, drained and cubed**
- **2 green onions, sliced**
- **3oz bean sprouts**

Cut noodles into 2-inch lengths. Place noodles in medium heatproof bowl, cover with boiling water, let stand until just tender; drain.

Blend miso with 1 cup of the water; strain into small bowl.

Add remaining water to large pan with dashi; stir until dissolved. Add noodles; bring to boil then remove from heat. Stir in miso mixture; add tofu.

Divide onions and sprouts among serving bowls; ladle in hot soup.

SERVES 4 TO 6

Must be made just before serving

Opposite above Thai pumpkin soup
Opposite below Coconut chicken soup
Below Miso soup

VIETNAMESE BEEF NOODLE SOUP

Pho bo is Vietnam's national dish, served at any time of day, both at home and by street vendors. We used 1/2-inch wide fresh rice noodles, fresh banh pho. To slice beef into paper-thin pieces, cover with plastic wrap and freeze for 30 minutes or until just firm.

2 small fresh red chilis
1¹/2 tablespoons peanut oil
1 large onion, chopped
2 cloves garlic, crushed
1 medium carrot, chopped
1¹/2 tablespoon grated fresh ginger
4 cups beef stock
2 cups water
1 teaspoon black peppercorns
2 star anise
1¹/2 tablespoons fish sauce
1lb beef round steak, sliced thinly
14oz fresh rice noodles
4oz bean sprouts
3 green onions, sliced thickly
3 tablespoons fresh mint
1/2 medium lemon, quartered

Remove seeds and membranes from chilis; cut lengthwise into thin strips.

Heat oil in large pan; cook onion, garlic, carrot and ginger, stirring, until onion is soft. Stir in stock, water, pepper, star anise and sauce. Bring to boil; simmer, uncovered, 30 minutes.

Strain stock mixture through a double layer of cheesecloth into large pan; discard vegetables and cheesecloth. Bring stock to boil.

Meanwhile, divide chili, beef, noodles, sprouts, onions, mint and lemon among serving bowls; ladle in boiling stock.

SERVES 4

Vietnamese beef noodle soup must be made just before serving. Vegetable stock can be prepared 1 day ahead

Storage Covered, in refrigerator
Freeze Stock suitable

PRAWN LAKSA

This spicy Malaysian soup has become so commonplace that its name has made it into our everyday language. We used fresh thin egg noodles and dried rice stick noodles.

2lb large uncooked prawns
1¹/₂ tablespoons vegetable oil
3¹/₄ cups coconut milk
4 cups chicken stock
2 tablespoons lime juice
1 tablespoon brown sugar
1 tablespoon fish sauce
6 kaffir lime leaves, torn
4oz dried rice noodles
8oz fresh egg noodles
3oz bean sprouts
3 tablespoons fresh cilantro

LAKSA PASTE
2 teaspoons ground coriander seeds
2 teaspoons ground cumin
1 teaspoon ground turmeric
1 large onion, chopped
¹/₃ cup coconut milk
1¹/₂ tablespoons grated
   fresh ginger
4 cloves garlic, crushed
¹/₄ cup finely chopped
   fresh lemon grass
2 small fresh red chilis,
   seeded, chopped
6 macadamias, chopped
1¹/₂ tablespoons shrimp paste

Shell and devein prawns, leaving tails on.

Heat oil in large pan; cook Laksa Paste, stirring, until fragrant. Stir in milk, stock, juice, sugar, sauce and lime leaves. Bring to boil; simmer, covered, 30 minutes.

Place rice noodles in medium heatproof bowl, cover with boiling water, let stand until just tender; drain.

Cook egg noodles in large pan of boiling salted water, uncovered, only until just tender; drain.

Stir prawns into soup mixture; simmer, uncovered, about 5 minutes or just until prawns change color.

Just before serving, divide both types of noodles among serving bowls. Ladle hot soup into each bowl; top with sprouts and cilantro.

Laksa Paste Blend or process all ingredients until smooth.

SERVES 4 TO 6

Prawn laksa must be made just before serving. Laksa paste can be prepared 3 days ahead

Storage Covered, tightly, in refrigerator
Freeze Laksa paste suitable

Opposite Vietnamese beef noodle soup
Right Prawn laksa

HOT AND SOUR SEAFOOD SOUP

The tangy Thai soup, tom yum goong, has become a firm favorite worldwide. We used a fresh wheat noodle traditionally made by hand in Asia but available ready-made here.

1¹/₂lb large uncooked prawns
8oz firm white fish fillets
1¹/₂ tablespoons peanut oil
1 large onion, sliced
6 green onions, chopped
4 cloves garlic, crushed
1¹/₂ tablespoons grated
    fresh ginger
2 teaspoons sambal oelek
1¹/₂ tablespoons finely chopped
    fresh lemon grass
2 kaffir lime leaves, torn
3 tablespoons tamarind concentrate
2 teaspoons sugar
3 tablespoons fish sauce
4 cups water
2 cups chicken stock
3 tablespoons tomato paste
8oz fresh wheat noodles
3 tablespoons shredded
    fresh cilantro
3 tablespoons shredded fresh mint
1oz bean sprouts

Shell and devein prawns. Cut fish into ³/₄-inch pieces.

Heat oil in large pan; cook both types of onions, garlic, ginger, sambal oelek, lemon grass and lime leaves, stirring, until onions are soft. Stir in tamarind, sugar, sauce, water, stock and paste;

bring to boil. Add noodles, return to boil; simmer, uncovered, 1 minute. Add herbs, prawns and fish; simmer, uncovered, about 3 minutes or until seafood is just cooked and noodles just tender.

Ladle soup into serving bowls; top with sprouts.

SERVES 4 TO 6

Best made just before serving

CHICKEN NOODLE SOUP

This Asian-influenced version of your homemade cold-remedy soup will inspire you. Try using the spaghetti-like fresh rice stick noodles to retain the soup's delicacy.

1 whole chicken (2¹/₂lb)
3 quarts cold water
¹/₂ teaspoon black peppercorns
1 stalk celery, chopped
1 medium leek, chopped
2 kaffir lime leaves, torn
2 dried bay leaves
1¹/₄ cups fresh cilantro, chopped
2-inch piece (3oz) fresh
  galangal, chopped
1 large corn cob, trimmed
4oz fresh rice noodles

Combine chicken, water, pepper, celery, leek, all leaves and galangal in large pan. Bring to boil; simmer, uncovered, 50 minutes or until chicken is tender.

Remove chicken from pan; discard skin and bones. Shred chicken finely; cover to keep warm. Strain stock into large pan.

Cut kernels from corn; add to stock. Bring to boil; simmer, uncovered, 10 minutes or until stock is reduced by about a quarter.

Cook noodles in another large pan of boiling salted water, uncovered, until just tender; drain.

Divide chicken and noodles among serving bowls; ladle in hot soup.

SERVES 4 TO 6

Best made just before serving

◰ **FRESH RICE NOODLES**, also known as ho fun or fan in China and sen yai in Thailand, are the noodles upon which Vietnamese pho, Malaysian char kway teow and Thai pad seew have built their reputations. Fresh rice noodles are made daily in Asia and, at night, noodle vendors have a happy hour when remaining stock sells at a cheaper rate, as it can ferment if left overnight. Refrigerate these noodles and use as soon as possible after purchase.

HEARTY SZECHUAN BEEF SOUP

Hokkien mee — fresh wheat noodles — are sold in most supermarkets these days.

1 teaspoon finely chopped or
  ground fresh lemon grass
2 cloves garlic, crushed
2 teaspoons coriander seeds
1¹/₂ teaspoons Szechuan pepper
1lb whole piece beef round steak
1¹/₂ tablespoons sweet chili sauce
3 tablespoons peanut oil
1lb Hokkien mee
1¹/₂ inches fresh ginger, sliced thinly
8 cups beef stock
2 teaspoons ketjap manis or a thick
  teriyaki sauce
1oz bean sprouts
¹/₄ cup fresh cilantro

Using a mortar and pestle, a blender or a new electric coffee grinder, crush lemon grass, garlic, seeds and pepper until almost smooth.

Combine spice mixture, beef, sauce and half the oil in medium bowl. Cover; refrigerate 3 hours or overnight.

Rinse noodles under hot water; drain. Transfer to large bowl; separate noodles with fork.

Cook beef on heated oiled griddle (or grill or barbecue) until browned both sides and cooked as desired. Slice beef thinly; cover to keep warm.

Heat remaining oil in large pan; cook ginger, stirring, until fragrant. Add stock and ketjap manis or a thick teriyaki sauce; bring to boil. Simmer; add noodles, stir until hot.

Ladle hot soup into serving bowls; top with beef, sprouts and cilantro.

SERVES 4 TO 6

Best made just before serving

Opposite above Hot and sour seafood soup
Opposite below Chicken noodle soup
Above Hearty Szechuan beef soup

MOROCCAN LAMB AND LENTIL SOUP

Harira, the Moroccan soup, is traditionally served as one of the dishes that breaks the daily fasting of the month-long Muslim observance of Ramadan. We added fresh thin egg noodles to further satisfy your hunger.

- 3 tablespoons olive oil
- 4 (1³/₄lb) trimmed lamb shanks
- 2 medium red onions, chopped
- 3 cloves garlic, crushed
- 1¹/₂ tablespoons ground cumin
- 1 teaspoon ground turmeric
- 2 teaspoons paprika
- ¹/₄ teaspoon ground cinnamon
- 6 medium tomatoes, peeled, seeded, chopped
- 2 9oz cans garbanzos, rinsed, drained
- ¹/₃ cup red lentils, rinsed, drained
- 6 cups chicken stock
- 13oz fresh egg noodles
- 3 tablespoons chopped fresh cilantro
- 2 tablespoons lemon juice

Heat oil in large pan; cook lamb until browned all over. Drain on paper towel. Cook onions, garlic and ground spices in same pan, stirring, 5 minutes. Return lamb to pan with tomatoes, garbanzos, lentils and stock. Bring to boil; simmer, covered, 2 hours or until lamb comes away from the bone, stirring occasionally. Remove lamb from pan; when cool enough to handle, pull lamb away from bones, discard bones. Chop lamb finely.

Cut noodles into 1-inch lengths. Return lamb to pan; bring to boil. Add noodles, cilantro and juice; boil, uncovered, until noodles are just tender.

SERVES 8

Best made just before serving

LONG AND SHORT SOUP

A favorite with many families, the combination of long noodles, a symbol of long life, and wontons, meat-filled dumplings in a clear broth, makes a meal in a bowl. We used dried rice stick noodles.

5 dried shiitake mushrooms
1lb large uncooked prawns
6 cups chicken stock
1 cup shredded Chinese (or napa) cabbage
¼ cup light soy sauce
¼ cup dry sherry
3½ oz dried rice noodles
3 green onions, sliced
1oz bean sprouts
1½ tablespoons chopped fresh cilantro

WONTONS

2oz boneless chicken breast, chopped
2oz ground pork
1 clove garlic, crushed
1 teaspoon grated fresh ginger
1½ tablespoon plum sauce
12 wonton wrappers
1 egg, beaten

Place mushrooms in small heatproof bowl, cover with boiling water, let stand 20 minutes; drain. Discard stems; slice caps thinly. Shell and devein prawns, leaving tails intact.

Bring stock to boil in large pan. Add mushrooms, cabbage, sauce, sherry and wontons; return to boil, then simmer, uncovered, 5 minutes. Add noodles and prawns; simmer until prawns change color. Stir in remaining ingredients.

Wontons Blend or process chicken, pork, garlic, ginger and sauce until mixture forms a paste. Place rounded teaspoons of mixture in center of wonton wrappers; brush edges lightly with egg. Bring opposite corners into center of wonton wrapper, press along edges to seal.

SERVES 4

Long and short soup best made just before serving. Wonton filling and stock can be prepared 1 day ahead

Storage Covered, separately, in refrigerator

Opposite Moroccan lamb and lentil soup
Above Long and short soup

Just for starters

◼ Whether you're after a curtain-raiser to the main course, finger food to serve at parties, or a range of delectable morsels to be accompanied by salad for a buffet lunch or supper, this treasure trove of recipes should satisfy most appetites and occasions. Noodles provide fabulous textures and the season's finest produce contributes a party of flavors to a stimulating celebration for the taste buds.

VIETNAMESE RICE-PAPER ROLLS

These beautiful bites are a healthy alternative to the usual spring roll. Goi cuon are traditionally made with pork belly and prawns but we've gone for a lighter approach with chicken and mung bean thread noodles.

3oz bean thread noodles
1^1/$_2$ tablespoons peanut oil
1^1/$_4$lb boneless chicken breasts
^{1}/$_3$ cup peanut oil, extra
1 teaspoon sesame oil
^{1}/$_3$ cup mirin
3 tablespoons finely chopped
    fresh lemon grass
2 teaspoons fish sauce
2 teaspoons ketjap manis or thick
    teriyaki sauce
1^1/$_2$ tablespoons chopped
    fresh ginger
2 cloves garlic, crushed
^{1}/$_2$ cup shredded fresh mint
1 small red onion, sliced
^{1}/$_2$ cup cashews, toasted, chopped
3oz bean sprouts
3 tablespoons grated lime rind
4 small fresh red chilis,
    seeded, chopped
16 9-inch round rice paper sheets
16 fresh mint leaves
^{1}/$_2$ cup mirin, extra
^{1}/$_4$ cup ketjap manis, or thick
    teriyaki sauce, extra
^{1}/$_3$ cup lime juice

Place noodles in small heatproof bowl, cover with boiling water, let stand only until just tender; drain. Cut noodles into 1^1/$_2$-inch lengths.

Heat peanut oil in medium pan; cook chicken until tender and browned both sides. Cut chicken into thin slices.

Combine extra peanut oil, sesame oil, mirin, lemon grass, fish sauce, ketjap manis, ginger, garlic and mint in large bowl; stir in noodles, chicken, onion, cashews, sprouts, rind and chili. Cover; refrigerate filling 30 minutes.

Place 1 sheet of rice paper in medium bowl of warm water until just softened; lift from water carefully, place on board. Place 1 mint leaf in center of rice paper; top with 1^1/$_2$ rounded tablespoons filling. Roll to enclose, folding in ends (roll should be about 3 inches long). Repeat with remaining rice paper sheets, mint and filling.

Combine remaining extra mirin, extra ketjap manis and lime juice in small bowl; serve as a dipping sauce with rolls.

MAKES 16

Can be made 3 hours ahead

Storage Rice-paper rolls and sauce, covered, separately, in refrigerator

▦ A pie plate of water also works well for softening rice paper sheets.
▦ Mirin is a sweet white wine made from fermented rice. It is Japanese in origin and can usually be found in the ethnic food section of grocery stores or in Asian specialty shops.

LION HEADS WITH BEAN-THREAD CRUNCH

We used mung bean thread noodles rather than grains of rice for the mane of our lions.

1lb ground chicken
1/4 cup chopped pistachios, toasted
2 cloves garlic, crushed
2 teaspoons ground cumin
2 teaspoons grated lemon rind
1/2 cup corn kernels, drained
1 cup fresh breadcrumbs
1 egg, beaten
1/2 cup cornstarch
1 egg, beaten, extra
1/2 cup milk
7oz bean thread noodles, crushed
vegetable oil, for deep-frying

ROASTED SWEET RED PEPPER SAUCE
2 medium sweet red bell peppers
1/2 cup cream
3 tablespoons coarsely grated parmesan cheese
1 clove garlic, chopped coarsely

GINGERY FRIED BEAN-CURD POUCHES WITH WASABI

We used mung bean thread noodles in our version of this popular sushi snack.

3oz bean thread noodles
1/3 cup seasoned rice vinegar
10 green onions
1/2 English cucumber
10 pouches prepared fried bean curd (or inarizushi)
2 tablespoons pickled ginger, drained
2 teaspoons wasabi
1/4 cup peanut oil
1/4 teaspoon sesame oil
1 teaspoon soy sauce
1/2 teaspoon sugar

Above Gingery fried bean-curd pouches with wasabi
Opposite above Sea scallops in black-bean sauce
Right Lion heads with bean-thread crunch

Place noodles in large heatproof bowl, cover with boiling water, let stand only until just tender; drain. Rinse under cold water; drain. Return noodles to same bowl; stir in half the vinegar. Line tray with plastic wrap, spread noodles on tray; cover, refrigerate until cold.

Meanwhile, cut green tops from onions to measure about 10 inches in length. Place tops in small heatproof bowl, cover with boiling water, let stand 5 minutes; drain. Rinse under cold water; drain.

Cut cucumber in thin, 2-inch strips. Gently open out bean-curd pieces to form pouches. Divide noodles among pouches; divide cucumber, ginger and half the wasabi on top of noodles in pouches.

Tie onion tops around pouches to secure filling; trim ends of onion tops. Drizzle pouches with combined remaining vinegar and wasabi, both oils, sauce and sugar.

MAKES 10

Can be prepared 1 day ahead

Storage Covered, in refrigerator

Combine chicken, nuts, garlic, cumin, rind, corn, breadcrumbs and egg in large bowl. Cover; refrigerate 1 hour.

Roll level tablespoons of chicken mixture into balls; roll in cornstarch, shake off excess. Dip chicken balls in combined extra egg and milk; roll balls in noodles. Heat oil in large pan; deep-fry lion heads, in batches, until cooked through. Drain lion heads on paper towels; serve warm with Roasted Sweet Red Pepper Sauce.

Roasted Sweet Red Pepper Sauce Quarter sweet red bell peppers remove seeds and membranes. Roast pepper pieces under broiler or in 500°F oven, skin-side up, until skin blisters and blackens. Wrap pepper pieces in plastic or paper, 5 minutes; peel away skin.

Blend or process peppers with cream, cheese and garlic until smooth. Transfer mixture to small pan; stir over heat until hot.

MAKES 30

Lion heads can be prepared up to 3 hours before deep-frying. Roasted Sweet Red Pepper Sauce can be made 1 day ahead

Storage Covered, separately, in refrigerator
Freeze Sauce suitable

SCALLOPS IN BLACK-BEAN SAUCE

Any dried rice noodle can be deep-fried for this recipe; we used a slightly wider variety so that the noodle pillows appear sturdy enough to support the scallops.

vegetable oil, for deep-frying
1¹/₂ oz dried rice noodles
1¹/₂ tablespoons salted black beans
2 teaspoons peanut oil
1 clove garlic, crushed
1 teaspoon grated fresh ginger
2 teaspoons light soy sauce
2 teaspoons hoisin sauce
1lb large scallops
8oz snow peas, sliced thinly
2 green onions, sliced thinly

Heat vegetable oil in large pan; deep-fry noodles, in batches, until puffed. Drain noodles on paper towels.

Rinse beans under cold water 1 minute; drain. Mash beans lightly. Heat peanut oil in wok or large pan; stir-fry beans, garlic and ginger until fragrant. Add sauces and scallops; stir-fry until scallops are just tender. Add snow peas; stir-fry 1 minute.

Divide noodles among serving plates; top with scallop mixture and onions.

SERVES 4

Best made just before serving

▦ Sugar snaps, the edible pod peas, make an excellent substitution for snow peas and are slightly sweeter in flavor.

SALMON AND AVOCADO SUSHI

Our interpretation of that popular type of sushi known as a California roll is filled with green bean thread vermicelli rather than rice.

5oz bean thread noodles
5 sheets toasted nori
4oz sliced smoked salmon
1 medium avocado,
sliced thinly
1 teaspoon rice vinegar
1 teaspoon sugar
2 teaspoons wasabi

Place noodles in large heatproof bowl, cover with boiling water, let stand only until just tender; drain. Line tray with plastic wrap; spread noodles on tray. Cover; refrigerate until cold.

Place a sheet of nori, shiny-side down, with the long side towards you, on bamboo sushi mat. Spread one-fifth of the noodles over nori, leaving a 1 1/2-inch border on far side.

Make hollow in center of noodles; if noodles are too sticky, moisten fingers with a little rice vinegar.

Place one-fifth of the salmon and avocado in hollow as shown; brush with one-fifth of the combined vinegar, sugar and wasabi. Using bamboo mat as a guide, roll up nori from closest edge, pressing down firmly as you roll. Remove the mat carefully. Using sharp knife, trim edges, cut sushi roll into 6 pieces. Repeat with remaining ingredients.

MAKES 30

Salmon and avocado sushi can be made up to 30 minutes ahead

Storage Covered, in refrigerator

◧ **Nori** is one of several kinds of seaweed used in Japanese cooking and, increasingly, our own. Today, it is possible to buy it already toasted and cut into the specific size needed for rolled sushi. Store it, airtight, in the freezer.

SANG CHOY BOW
REVISITED

*Here's a twist on the classic Chinese sang
choy bow: we've provided fresh spinach
leaves for wrapping the pork mixture in
place of the traditional iceberg lettuce.*

2oz bean thread noodles
2lb spinach
1¹/₂ tablespoons peanut oil
1lb ground pork
2 cloves garlic, crushed
3 green onions, chopped
3 tablespoons light soy sauce
3¹/₂ tablespoons seasoned
rice vinegar
1 tablespoon sambal oelek
¹/₂ teaspoon sesame oil
2 teaspoons grated lime rind
2 tablespoons lime juice
3 tablespoons chopped
fresh cilantro

Place noodles in small heatproof
bowl, cover with boiling water, let stand
only until just tender; drain well. Cut
noodles into 1¹/₂-inch lengths.

Trim and discard stems from spinach;
wash thoroughly, pat dry.

Heat peanut oil in wok or large pan;
stir-fry pork, garlic and onions until well
browned. Add sauce, vinegar, sambal
oelek, sesame oil, rind and juice; stir-fry
2 minutes. Stir in noodles and cilantro.

Just before serving, place pork filling
in bowl on serving platter; place spinach
leaves around pork mixture. Each person
spoons a little pork filling onto a spinach
leaf then rolls leaf to enclose.

SERVES 8 TO 10

Best made on day of serving

Storage Covered, in refrigerator
Freeze Pork filling suitable

▭ **BEAN THREAD NOODLES** are called
wun sen in Thailand and fun si in China.
They look similar to vermicelli-type dried
rice noodles but are tougher. They are
quite hard to cut — use a cleaver but be
very careful not to injure your hands.
Better still, buy the kind that are sold
tied in serving-sized bundles. Most recipes
require them to be softened by soaking in
boiling water in a heatproof bowl for a
few minutes. They can also be deep-fried
to form puffed parcels.

Opposite Salmon and avocado sushi
Above Sang choy bow revisited

NOODLE BUNDLES

This recipe can also serve as an accompaniment to main courses. We used the Japanese wheat flour noodle, udon, because of its supple qualities.

7oz udon
12 green onions

Cook noodles in large pan of boiling water, uncovered, until just tender; drain. Rinse under cold water; drain. Spread noodles in thin layer on tray; allow to cool.

Cut green tops from onions to measure about 10 inches in length. Place tops in small heatproof bowl, cover with boiling water, let stand 5 minutes; drain. Rinse under cold water; drain.

Shape noodles into 12 bundles; tie with onion tops. Trim any loose bits of noodles or onion tops.

MAKES 12

Best made on day of serving

Storage Covered, in refrigerator

LIME CHILI SAUCE

Both this sauce and the following one can be used with any one of the three recipes on this page or, indeed, all of them. The noodle bundles, in particular, are lovely eaten just as they are when accompanied by this tart, tangy sauce.

1 small fresh red chili,
chopped finely
1/4 cup lime juice
3 tablespoons brown sugar
1 1/2 tablespoons fish sauce
1 teaspoon finely chopped
fresh lemon grass

Combine ingredients in jar; shake well.

MAKES 1/2 CUP

Can be made 1 day ahead

Storage Covered, in refrigerator

PEANUT CHILI SAUCE

Sweet chili and peanut sauce is associated with Thai food, and this one goes really well with grilled meats.

1/3 cup sweet chili sauce
1 1/2 tablespoons chopped
roasted peanuts
1 1/2 tablespoons chopped
fresh cilantro

Combine ingredients in jar; shake well.

MAKES 1/2 CUP

Can be made 1 day ahead

Storage Covered, in refrigerator

CRISP PRAWNS

Try this different coating when frying a firm fish or chicken: crush a fine to medium width mung bean noodle.

18 (2lb) medium
uncooked prawns
all-purpose flour
1 egg, beaten
1/2 cup milk
3 1/2 oz bean thread
noodles, crushed
1 1/2 tablespoons chopped
fresh cilantro
peanut oil, for deep-frying

Shell and devein prawns, leaving tails intact. Roll prawns in flour; shake off excess. Dip prawns in combined egg and milk, then combined noodles and cilantro.

Heat oil in large pan; deep-fry prawns, in batches, until browned and crisp. Drain prawns on paper towels.

MAKES 18

Best made just before serving

RED CURRY NOODLE PANCAKES

Pancakes may be served room temperature or hot. We used thin rice vermicelli as part of the batter.

3oz dried rice noodles
2 green onions
1/2 cup all-purpose flour
2 eggs, beaten
1/4 cup coconut milk
1/4 cup red curry paste
peanut oil, for frying

Place noodles in small heatproof bowl, cover with boiling water, let stand until just tender; drain. Cut noodles into 2-inch lengths.

Remove green tops of onions; save for another use. Finely chop white portions.

Stir noodles and onions in medium bowl with combined flour, eggs, milk and paste.

Heat oil in large pan; fry level tablespoons of mixture, in batches, until browned and cooked through. Drain on paper towels.

MAKES ABOUT 18

Can be prepared 3 hours ahead

Storage Covered, in refrigerator

Clockwise from top left Crisp prawns; Red curry noodle pancakes; Peanut chili sauce; Lime chili sauce; Noodle bundles

NOODLY CHICKEN SAMOSAS WITH PEANUT SAMBAL

We used green bean thread vermicelli inside these Indian-style snacks.

8oz butternut squash, chopped
1 medium potato, chopped
3 1/2 oz bean thread noodles
1 1/2 tablespoons vegetable oil
1lb boneless chicken breasts
1 medium onion, chopped
2 cloves garlic, crushed
2 teaspoons curry powder
6 puff pastry sheets, thawed
1 egg, beaten
peanut oil, for deep-frying

PEANUT SAMBAL
8 green onions, chopped
3 small fresh red chilis, seeded, chopped
1/3 cup lime juice
1 1/2 tablespoons peanut oil
1 1/3 cups unsalted roasted peanuts
1 2/3 cups coconut milk
2 teaspoons tamarind concentrate
1/2 cup water
1 1/2 tablespoons brown sugar

Boil, steam or microwave squash and potato, separately, until tender; drain, mash together in large bowl.

Place noodles in medium heatproof bowl, cover with boiling water, stand until just tender; drain. Chop noodles coarsely; stir into mashed vegetables.

Heat vegetable oil in medium pan; cook chicken until tender. Chop chicken; add to noodle filling. Cook onion, garlic and curry powder in same pan, stirring, until onion is soft; add to noodle filling.

Using a 3 1/2-inch cookie cutter, cut 4 rounds from each pastry sheet. Place heaping tablespoons of noodle filling in center of each round. Brush edges of pastry with a little egg; fold over, pinch edges firmly together to seal. Place samosas on tray, cover; refrigerate 1 hour.

Heat oil in large pan; deep-fry puffs, in batches, until lightly browned. Drain samosas on paper towels. Serve with Peanut Sambal.

Peanut Sambal Blend or process onions, chilis, juice, oil and peanuts until combined. Add combined remaining ingredients to medium pan; stir in peanut mixture. Bring mixture to boil; simmer, uncovered, about 4 minutes or until thickened slightly.

MAKES 24

Samosa filling and peanut sambal can be made 1 day ahead

Storage Covered, separately, in refrigerator
Freeze Uncooked samosas suitable

VEGETABLE AND RAMEN FRITTERS

Ramen, dried wheat noodles, are sometimes referred to as instant or 2-minute noodles in reference to their short cooking time. We used a straight version of ramen here.

3 1/2 oz ramen
1 1/2 tablespoons peanut oil
1 medium onion, chopped
2 cloves garlic, crushed
2 teaspoons grated fresh ginger
1 tablespoon black mustard seeds
1 tablespoon ground coriander
1 tablespoon ground cumin
1/2 teaspoon ground turmeric
1 medium carrot, grated coarsely
1 medium potato, grated coarsely, drained
1/2 cup chicken stock
4 eggs, beaten
3/4 cup yogurt
1 1/2 tablespoons lime juice
1 1/2 tablespoons chopped fresh mint
2oz baby spinach leaves
2 medium tomatoes, peeled, seeded, chopped

Cook noodles in large pan of boiling, salted water, uncovered, until just tender; drain. Rinse under cold water; drain.

Heat oil in medium pan; cook onion, garlic and ginger, stirring, until onion is soft. Add mustard seeds and spices; cook, stirring, until seeds pop. Add carrot and potato; cook until soft, stirring occasionally. Stir in stock, bring to boil; simmer, uncovered, until almost all liquid evaporates. Cool.

Combine noodles and vegetable mixture in large bowl with eggs. Cook 1/3 cupfuls of mixture in heated oiled medium non-stick pan, in batches, until browned both sides and cooked through.

Meanwhile, combine yogurt, juice and mint in small bowl. Serve yogurt sauce with fritters topped with spinach and tomatoes.

SERVES 4

Yogurt sauce can be prepared 1 day ahead

Storage Covered, in refrigerator

CHILI CHICKEN PATTIES WITH LIME SAUCE

Any dried rice stick noodle can be crushed for the coating in this recipe; we chose to use a flat, fairly wide bean thread noodle.

2oz dried rice noodles, crushed
1¹/₂lb ground chicken
**2 teaspoons finely chopped
   fresh lemon grass**
2 teaspoons chopped fresh red chili
1 teaspoon finely grated lime rind
**3 tablespoons chopped
   fresh cilantro**
all-purpose flour
3 tablespoons peanut oil
1/3 cup lime juice
3 tablespoons fish sauce
3 tablespoons brown sugar
1/4 cup dry white wine
1/3 cup sweet chili sauce

Place noodles in small heatproof bowl, cover with boiling water, let stand until just tender; drain.

Combine noodles with chicken, lemon grass, chili, rind and half the cilantro in large bowl. Shape 1/4 cupfuls of mixture into patties; roll in flour, shake off excess.

Heat oil in large pan; cook patties, in batches, until browned both sides and cooked through.

Combine remaining ingredients in jar; shake lime sauce well. Serve chicken patties with the lime sauce.

MAKES 14

Uncooked chili chicken patties and sauce can be prepared 1 day ahead

Storage Covered, separately, in refrigerator
Freeze Uncooked patties suitable

◧ **RAMEN** is a crinkly or straight dried wheat noodle and a popular fast food in Japan where ramen bars are traditionally run by Chinese. Ramen was immortalized in the film *Tampopo* which tells the story of two truck drivers' quest to find the best ramen-maker in Japan. Sold in cakes, it is very popular in soups.

Opposite Noodly chicken samosas with peanut sambal
Above Vegetable and ramen fritters
Below Chili chicken patties with lime sauce

MINI SPRING ROLLS WITH CHILI CUCUMBER SAUCE

Thin wheat noodles, almost like vermicelli, make a surprise appearance in this recipe.

4 dried shiitake mushrooms
3¹/2 oz dried wheat noodles
1 clove garlic, crushed
1 teaspoon grated fresh ginger
4 green onions, sliced
¹/2 medium carrot, sliced thinly
1oz bean sprouts
2 teaspoons oyster sauce
2 teaspoons cornstarch
2 teaspoons water
24 5-inch square spring roll wrappers
peanut oil, for deep-frying

CHILI CUCUMBER SAUCE
1 cucumber, chopped finely
¹/4 cup sweet chili sauce
1 small tomato, peeled, seeded, chopped
1 teaspoon light soy sauce
1 clove garlic, crushed

Place mushrooms in small heatproof bowl, cover with boiling water, allow to stand 20 minutes; drain. Discard stems; slice caps thinly.

Cook noodles in large pan of boiling, salted water, uncovered, until just tender; drain. Rinse under cold water; drain. Cut noodles into 2¹/2-inch lengths.

Combine mushrooms and noodles in large bowl with garlic, ginger, onions, carrot, sprouts and sauce. Blend cornstarch with water in small bowl.

Spoon 1 rounded tablespoon of noodle mixture across a corner of one wrapper. Lightly brush edges of wrapper with a little cornstarch mixture; roll to enclose filling, folding in ends. Roll should be 2¹/2 inches long. Repeat with remaining noodle mixture, wrappers and cornstarch mixture.

Just before serving, heat oil in large pan; deep-fry spring rolls, in batches, until golden brown and cooked through. Drain spring rolls on paper towels; serve with Chili Cucumber Sauce.

Chili Cucumber Sauce Reserve ¹/4 cup cucumber. Blend or process remaining ingredients until smooth. Stir in reserved amount of cucumber.

MAKES 24

Filling and Chili cucumber sauce can be made 3 hours ahead. Mini spring rolls can be prepared 30 minutes before deep-frying; cover with slightly damp cloth.

Storage Covered, separately, in refrigerator
Freeze Uncooked rolls suitable

JAPANESE CHILLED NOODLES

Zaru-soba, a firm favorite in Japan's summers, is traditionally served on a bamboo mat fitted inside a tray or platter to allow any liquid to drain away from the noodles.

8oz soba
2 sheets nori, toasted, shredded
2 green onions, chopped finely
¹/4 cup pickled ginger
2 tablespoons wasabi

DIPPING SAUCE
¹/2 cup dark soy sauce
¹/4 cup mirin
1 teaspoon sugar
¹/2 teaspoon dashi granules
1¹/4 cups water
¹/2 oz dried bonito flakes

Cook noodles in large pan of boiling, salted water, uncovered, until just tender; drain. Rinse under cold water; drain. Cover; refrigerate at least 3 hours or until cold.

Divide noodles among 4 bamboo baskets; sprinkle with nori. Place onions, ginger, wasabi and Dipping Sauce in separate bowls; serve with noodles.

Dipping Sauce Combine sauce, mirin, sugar, dashi and water in medium pan. Bring to boil, add flakes; remove from heat. Strain into large heatproof bowl; discard flakes. Cover; refrigerate sauce until cold.

SERVES 4

Best made on day of serving

▭ **ZARU-SOBA** is considered by many the connoisseur's soba as the merits of the noodles virtually stand alone. The origin of the name goes back 300 years, when soba was made by confectioners. Noodles made of 100% buckwheat broke easily, so the sweetmakers steamed and served them in take-zaru, bamboo baskets. Today, wheat flour is mixed with buckwheat to strengthen the noodles so they can be boiled, but the tradition of the bamboo basket remains, along with the name.

Below Mini spring rolls with chili cucumber sauce
Opposite Japanese chilled noodles

STEAMED PORK DUMPLINGS WITH PLUM SAUCE

Peking noodles were our choice for this classic pork and plum combination. You have to use noodles of the same length to achieve a neat result.

2 dried shiitake mushrooms
1lb ground pork
2 green onions, chopped
2 cloves garlic, crushed
2 teaspoons grated fresh ginger
1¹/₂ cups fresh breadcrumbs
3 tablespoons light soy sauce
1¹/₂ tablespoons hoisin sauce
1 egg, beaten
3 tablespoons chopped
  fresh cilantro
1lb Peking noodles
1¹/₄lb choy sum, halved
¹/₂ cup plum sauce
1 teaspoon sesame oil
¹/₃ cup chicken stock
1¹/₂ tablespoons chopped fresh
  cilantro, extra

Place mushrooms in small heatproof bowl, cover with boiling water, let stand 20 minutes; drain. Discard stems; chop caps finely.

Combine mushrooms, pork, onion, garlic, ginger, breadcrumbs, sauces, egg and cilantro in large bowl. Shape rounded tablespoons of pork mixture into dumplings; place on tray. Cover; refrigerate 30 minutes.

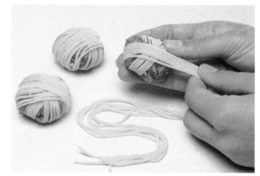

Place noodles in a single layer on work surface. Holding 5 or 6 noodles in your hand, wrap around each pork dumpling, as shown, finishing with noodle ends at the base.

Place dumplings, in single layer, about ³/4 inch apart, in bamboo steamer lined with parchment. Cook, covered, over wok or large pan of simmering water until dumplings are cooked through, brushing noodles with a little water occasionally.

Meanwhile, boil, steam or microwave choy sum until wilted; drain. Rinse under cold water; drain.

Combine remaining ingredients in small pan, stir plum sauce until hot. Serve dumplings over choy sum with plum sauce.

SERVES 4 TO 6

Uncooked pork dumplings and plum sauce can be prepared 1 day ahead

Storage Covered, separately, in refrigerator
Microwave Plum sauce suitable

LAMB DOLMADES

Again, noodles replace rice in another traditional dish – this time, a Mediterranean favorite. We used extremely fine dried rice noodles here.

4oz dried rice noodles, crushed
1¹/₂ tablespoons olive oil
1¹/₂lb ground lamb
1 large onion, chopped
2 cloves garlic, crushed
2 teaspoons ground cumin
¹/₂ teaspoon grated lemon rind
¹/₄ cup all-purpose flour
¹/₃ cup water
7oz grape leaves in brine

TOMATO SAUCE
1¹/₂ tablespoons olive oil
1 large onion, chopped
1 clove garlic, crushed
2 14oz cans tomatoes
1 tablespoon chopped fresh mint

Place noodles in bowl, cover with boiling water, let stand until just tender; drain.

Heat oil in large pan; cook lamb, stirring, until browned. Add onion and garlic; cook, stirring, until onion is soft. Stir in cumin, rind and flour; bring to boil, simmer, uncovered, about 10 minutes or until lamb mixture is thickened. Cool. Stir in noodles and water. Rinse grape leaves under cold water; drain, pat dry.

Place rounded tablespoons of lamb mixture in center of each grape leaf. Fold in sides of leaf; roll up tightly to enclose filling. Place rolls close together in base of 2-quart ovenproof dish. Cover with Tomato Sauce; bake, covered, at 350°F for 30 minutes.

Tomato Sauce Heat oil in large pan; cook onion and garlic, stirring, until soft. Stir in undrained, crushed tomatoes and mint. Bring to boil; simmer, uncovered, about 10 minutes or until tomatoes are soft.

SERVES 4 TO 6

Lamb dolmades can be made 1 day ahead

Storage Covered, in refrigerator
Freeze Lamb mixture suitable

◼ **PEKING NOODLES** are a fresh wheat noodle, made without egg. These thin, rather square, caramel-colored noodles resemble the Italian pasta, linguine, and are extremely soft and malleable. They can be purchased in supermarkets and Asian food stores, fresh, in vacuum-packs.

Opposite Steamed pork dumplings with plum sauce
Below Lamb dolmades

Prime-time salads

Gone are the days of the salad as a bowl of tossed greens which, no matter how you dressed it up, smacked of deprivation. This round-up of recipes introduces the new-age salad as a stand-alone sensation, its delicious combinations guaranteed to turn even the most rabid salad-haters into aficionados. You'd make them just to taste but there's a bonus – they're good for you as well.

SMOKED SALMON, AVOCADO AND UDON SALAD

We used udon, the delectable wide, white, Japanese wheat noodle, in this light salad.

8oz udon
10oz sliced smoked salmon
3oz snow pea sprouts
2 tablespoons chopped fresh chives
1 small red onion, chopped finely
2 small avocados, chopped finely
$1/3$ cup light olive oil
3 tablespoons seasoned rice vinegar
$1^1/_2$ tablespoons mirin
$1^1/_2$ tablespoons lime juice
2 teaspoons wasabi

Cook noodles in large pan of boiling salted water, uncovered, until just tender; drain. Rinse under cold water; drain.

Separate smoked salmon slices; cut into small strips. Just before serving, gently toss noodles and salmon in large bowl with sprouts, chives, onion, avocados and combined remaining ingredients.

SERVES 4 TO 6

Best made just before serving

LEMON-MARINATED TUNA SALAD

We used banh pho, wide Vietnamese rice stick noodles, in this salad but you can use whichever dried rice noodle you prefer, whether Chinese, Thai or Taiwanese.

**1lb piece fresh tuna steak
   split in half lengthwise**
1/3 cup olive oil
1 1/2 tablespoons grated lemon rind
1/2 cup lemon juice
1 teaspoon cracked black pepper
2 cloves garlic, crushed
7oz rice stick noodles
1 cup green beans
1 cup butter beans
1/3 cup olive oil, extra
3 tablespoons chopped fresh parsley
1 medium radicchio, trimmed

Combine tuna, oil, rind, juice, pepper and garlic in large bowl; cover, refrigerate at least 3 hours or overnight.

Place noodles in large heatproof bowl, cover with boiling water, let stand until just tender; drain. Rinse under cold water; drain. Boil, steam or microwave both beans until just tender; drain. Rinse under cold water; drain.

CHICKEN, CUCUMBER AND SPROUT SALAD

Locally manufactured fresh egg noodles were used here.

1 1/4 cups chicken stock
1/4 cup lime juice
1/4 cup dry white wine
3 (1lb) boneless chicken breasts
1 large cucumber
7oz fresh egg noodles
4oz bean sprouts
2 small fresh red chilis, seeded, sliced
**1 1/2 tablespoons chopped
   fresh cilantro**
1/4 cup light olive oil
2 tablespoons lime juice, extra
1 1/2 tablespoons sweet chili sauce
**1 1/2 tablespoons seasoned rice
   vinegar**
2 teaspoons hoisin sauce
1 teaspoon soy sauce

Combine stock, lime juice, wine and chicken in large pan. Bring to boil; simmer, covered, about 20 minutes or until chicken is just tender. Remove chicken from stock; when cool enough to handle, slice thinly.

Halve cucumber; remove seeds, slice diagonally. Cook noodles in large pan of boiling salted water, uncovered, until just tender; drain. Rinse under cold water; drain.

Gently toss chicken, cucumber and noodles in large bowl with bean sprouts, chilis, cilantro and combined remaining ingredients.

SERVES 6 TO 8

Can be prepared 1 day ahead

Storage Covered, in refrigerator
Microwave Chicken suitable

Above Chicken, cucumber and sprout salad
Right Lemon-marinated tuna salad
Opposite above Lime, tomato and scallop salad

Drain tuna into small bowl; reserve marinade. Cook tuna in large heated oiled pan about 3 minutes each side or until browned but still pink inside. Remove from pan, cover; let stand 5 minutes. Cut into 1/2-inch slices; cover to keep warm.

Transfer reserved marinade to same pan. Bring to boil; simmer, uncovered, 1 minute. Whisk in extra oil and parsley.

Gently toss tuna and noodles in large bowl with both beans, radicchio and warm marinade.

SERVES 4 TO 6

Lemon-marinated tuna salad best made just before serving. Tuna steak can be marinated 1 day ahead

Storage Covered, in refrigerator
Microwave Beans suitable

▬ **RICE STICK NOODLES** only differ from dried rice noodles in that they are thicker. The two noodles can easily be interchanged with the only sacrifice being appearance in a dish such as pad thai which is traditionally made with the broader noodle. Using a heatproof bowl, soak noodles to soften for about 4 to 8 minutes in boiling water before use. You might find them labeled ho fun on Chinese packets and sen lek in Thai.

LIME, TOMATO AND SCALLOP SALAD

The Thais use these ethereal rice stick noodles in their own cold noodle dishes.

8oz dried rice noodles
1lb large white scallops
1 1/2 tablespoons mild sweet chili sauce
1 1/2 tablespoons lime juice
8oz asparagus, trimmed, chopped
12oz yellow pear tomatoes, halved
1/3 cup slivered almonds, toasted

LIME DRESSING
1/2 cup peanut oil
1 teaspoon brown sugar
3 tablespoons chopped fresh cilantro
1 1/2 tablespoons chopped fresh mint
2 small fresh red chilis, seeded
1/4 cup lime juice

Place noodles in large heatproof bowl, cover with boiling water, let stand only until just tender; drain. Rinse under cold water; drain.

Cook scallops, in batches, on heated oiled griddle (or grill or barbecue) until changed in color, occasionally brushing with combined sauce and juice. Boil, steam or microwave asparagus until just tender; rinse under cold water, drain.

Gently toss noodles, scallops and asparagus in large bowl with tomatoes and Lime Dressing; sprinkle with almonds.

Lime Dressing Blend or process all ingredients until smooth.

SERVES 4

Best made just before serving

LAMB AND SPINACH SALAD

Beautiful Korean somyun noodles star here but you can substitute somen or even udon.

1lb boneless lamb tenderloin
3 tablespoons green peppercorns, drained, chopped finely
1½ tablespoons olive oil
8oz cherry tomatoes, halved
5oz dried wheat noodles
5oz feta cheese, chopped
8oz baby spinach leaves
1 clove garlic, chopped finely
1 teaspoon Dijon mustard
¼ cup white wine vinegar
1½ tablespoons chopped fresh rosemary
½ cup olive oil, extra

Roll lamb in green peppercorns. Heat 1 teaspoon of the oil in medium non-stick pan; cook lamb until browned all over and cooked as desired. Remove from pan, cover; let stand 5 minutes. Cut into ½-inch slices.

Place tomatoes in baking dish; drizzle with remaining oil. Bake, uncovered, at 450°F about 5 minutes or until just softened slightly.

Cook noodles in large pan of boiling salted water, uncovered, until just tender; drain. Rinse under cold water; drain.

Gently toss lamb, tomatoes and noodles in large bowl with feta, spinach and combined remaining ingredients.

SERVES 4

Lamb and spinach salad best made just before serving. Lamb and tomatoes can be prepared 1 day ahead

Storage Covered, separately, in refrigerator

FETA AND SWEET RED BELL PEPPER SALAD

Hokkien mee, a Chinese style egg noodle, is commonly thought of as the stir-fry noodle but here we eat it au naturel.

1lb Hokkien mee
2 large sweet red bell peppers
4 medium plum tomatoes
1½ tablespoons vegetable oil
5oz feta cheese
2 cups frozen fava beans, cooked, peeled
3 tablespoons fresh mint leaves, torn
1 small fresh red chili, seeded, chopped finely
1½ tablespoons chopped fresh cilantro
1 clove garlic, chopped finely
1½ tablespoons lime juice
1½ tablespoons balsamic vinegar
3 tablespoons sesame oil
3 tablespoons ketjap manis
2 teaspoons grated lime rind
2 teaspoons raw sugar

GRILLED VEGETABLE AND HALOUMI STACKS

Japanese soba come in many flavored varieties (gozen soba), one of which is cha-soba, made with powdered green tea as well as buckwheat, the essential ingredient. Substitute cha-soba with any kind of soba you can find, or even a thin wheat noodle.

1 medium eggplant
coarse cooking salt
2 medium sweet red bell peppers
3¹/2 oz cha-soba
2 medium yellow zucchini, sliced
2 medium green zucchini, sliced
7oz haloumi or fontina
    cheese, sliced
¹/4 cup olive oil
3 tablespoons balsamic vinegar
1 clove garlic, crushed
1¹/2 tablespoons chopped
    fresh oregano

Cut eggplant into ¹/2-inch slices, place on wire rack; sprinkle with salt, let stand 30 minutes. Rinse slices under cold water; pat dry.

Quarter peppers; remove seeds and membranes. Roast under broiler or in 500°F oven, skin-side up, until skin blisters and blackens. Wrap pepper pieces in plastic or paper for 5 minutes, peel away skin; cut each quarter in half.

Cook noodles in large pan of boiling salted water, uncovered, until just tender; drain. Rinse under cold water; drain.

Cook pepper and zucchini, on both sides, in batches, on heated oiled griddle (or grill or barbecue) until browned and just tender. Add cheese; cook, on both sides, about 30 seconds or until browned.

Layer vegetables, noodles and cheese in "stacks" on individual serving plates; drizzle with combined remaining ingredients.

SERVES 4

Best made just before serving

▭ STORAGE Fresh noodles of all kinds should be refrigerated until required and used as soon as possible after purchase. Dried noodles have much longer lives. Provided they are stored in unopened packets or airtight containers, they can sit happily on the pantry shelf for several months.

Rinse noodles under hot water; drain. Transfer to large bowl; separate noodles with a fork.

Quarter peppers; remove seeds and membranes. Roast under broiler or in a 500°F oven, skin-side up, until skin blisters and blackens. Wrap pepper pieces in plastic or paper for 5 minutes, peel away skin; slice into thin strips.

Cut each tomato in half lengthwise; place cut-side up on oven tray. Brush tomato halves with oil, grill 10 minutes or until browned and soft; cut each half into 2 wedges.

Dice cheese.

Just before serving, gently toss the noodles, pepper strips, tomatoes and cheese in large bowl with beans, mint and combined remaining ingredients.

SERVES 4

Feta and Sweet Red Bell Pepper salad best made just before serving. Sweet red bell peppers and tomatoes can be prepared 1 day ahead

Storage Covered, separately, in refrigerator

Opposite above Lamb and spinach salad
Opposite Feta and sweet red bell pepper salad
Above Grilled vegetable and haloumi stacks

SESAME BEEF SALAD

The use of Dijon mustard and honey gives a unique lift to this classic Asian dish.

1lb beef ribeye steak
1 teaspoon grated fresh ginger
1 clove garlic, crushed
1/4 cup light soy sauce
1/4 cup sweet sherry
3 tablespoons sesame oil
8oz asparagus, trimmed
5oz snow peas, trimmed
8oz dried wheat noodles
1 teaspoon Dijon mustard
2 teaspoons honey
1 tablespoon white wine vinegar
2 tablespoons olive oil
3 green onions, sliced
1¹/₂ tablespoons sesame seeds, toasted

Combine beef with ginger, garlic, soy sauce, sherry and sesame oil in large bowl. Cover; refrigerate 3 hours or overnight.

Cut asparagus into 1¹/₂-inch lengths. Boil, steam or microwave asparagus and snow peas, separately, until just tender;

HAZELNUT CHICKEN SALAD

The Chinese dried wheat noodle used here is labeled yolk noodle but, as is often the case with packaging translations, we suspect the pale yolky hue can be attributed more to food coloring than to an egg.

4 boneless chicken breasts
1 clove garlic, crushed
1¹/₂ tablespoons lime juice
3 tablespoons olive oil
6oz dried wheat noodles
4oz arugula, trimmed
7oz curly endive, trimmed
1/2 cup hazelnuts, toasted, chopped
1/4 cup raspberry vinegar
1¹/₂ tablespoons stone ground mustard
1/2 cup hazelnut oil

Combine chicken, garlic, lime juice and olive oil in large bowl. Cover; refrigerate 3 hours or overnight.

Cook chicken on heated oiled griddle (or grill or barbecue) until browned both sides and tender. Slice into 1-inch strips.

Cook noodles in large pan of boiling salted water, uncovered, until just tender; drain. Rinse under cold water; drain.

Gently toss chicken and noodles in large bowl with arugula, endive, nuts and combined remaining ingredients.

SERVES 4 TO 6

Hazelnut chicken salad best made just before serving. Chicken can be prepared 1 day ahead

Storage Covered, in refrigerator
Freeze Chicken suitable

drain. Rinse under cold water; drain.

Cook noodles in large pan of boiling salted water, uncovered, until just tender; drain. Rinse under cold water; drain.

Drain beef into small bowl; reserve marinade. Cook beef in large heated oiled pan until browned both sides and cooked as desired. Remove from pan; cool, then slice beef thinly. Add marinade to same pan. Bring to boil; simmer, uncovered, about 2 minutes or until the mixture thickens slightly.

Cool marinade then combine with mustard, honey, vinegar and olive oil in large bowl.

Just before serving, gently toss beef, asparagus, snow peas and noodles in large bowl with marinade mixture, onions and sesame seeds.

SERVES 4

Can be prepared 1 day ahead

Storage Covered, separately, in refrigerator

Opposite Hazelnut chicken salad
Below Sesame beef salad
Right Stringhopper salad

STRINGHOPPER SALAD

Stringhoppers are sometimes called Idly in Indian restaurants; look for them, dried, in both Indian and Sri Lankan shops.

1¹/2 tablespoons seasoned pepper
2lb whole piece beef round steak
4 slices bacon, chopped
vegetable oil, for deep-frying
3oz dried stringhoppers
4 hard-boiled eggs, quartered
5oz baby spinach leaves
8oz cherry tomatoes, halved
  (about 16)
8oz yellow pear tomatoes,
  halved (about 20-24)
ANCHOVY DRESSING

6 anchovy fillets, drained
1 clove garlic, crushed
2 teaspoons Dijon mustard
2 teaspoons white wine vinegar
1 teaspoon sugar
¹/2 cup olive oil
¹/2 cup buttermilk

Sprinkle pepper over beef. Cook beef on heated oiled griddle (or grill or barbecue) until browned on both sides and cooked as desired. Remove from pan; cover. Let stand 5 minutes; slice thinly.

Add bacon to same heated pan; cook, stirring, until crisp. Remove from pan; drain on paper towels.

Heat oil in large pan; deep-fry stringhoppers, in batches, until puffed. Drain stringhoppers on paper towels.

Gently toss beef and bacon in large bowl with eggs, spinach and tomatoes. Divide stringhoppers among 6 serving plates, top with beef mixture; drizzle with Anchovy Dressing.

Anchovy Dressing Blend or process anchovies, garlic, mustard, vinegar and sugar until almost smooth. With motor running, gradually pour in oil; process until thick. Add buttermilk; process until thickened slightly.

SERVES 6

Best made just before serving

SWEET CHILI PRAWN SALAD

Bean thread noodles are sometimes known as cellophane or glass noodles because of their fragile, transparent appearance.

vegetable oil, for deep-frying
3oz bean thread noodles
16 (1^1/$_2$lb) medium
    uncooked prawns
3 tablespoons sesame oil
2 cloves garlic, crushed
3 green onions, chopped
3oz bean sprouts
1 small sweet red bell pepper,
    seeded, sliced
1oz snow peas, sliced finely

SWEET CHILI SAUCE
6 small fresh red chilis,
    seeded, chopped
1^1/$_2$ tablespoons white raisins
1 clove garlic, crushed
1 teaspoon grated fresh ginger
1^1/$_2$ tablespoons white vinegar
^{1}/$_4$ cup sugar
^{1}/$_2$ teaspoon salt
^{1}/$_4$ cup water

Heat oil in large pan; deep-fry noodles, in batches, until puffed. Drain noodles on paper towels.

Shell and devein prawns, leaving tails intact. Heat sesame oil in wok or large pan; stir-fry garlic, onions, sprouts, pepper, snow peas and prawns until prawns are tender and change color.

Just before serving, gently toss prawn mixture and noodles in large bowl with Sweet Chili Sauce.

Sweet Chili Sauce Blend or process all ingredients until well combined; transfer to small pan. Bring to boil; simmer, uncovered, until sauce thickens slightly, stirring occasionally.

SERVES 4

Best made just before serving

⊏ **NOODLES** can replace rice, potatoes and other pastas in many of your favorite recipes, whether they're Asian in origin or not. Be daring, creative and ingenious with your cooking, and – who knows – one of your inventions could become a family favorite you make time and time again. And the world won't stop if one doesn't turn out to be perfect.

CRUNCHY COLESLAW WITH FRIED NOODLES

The fried noodles called for here are already prepared as crunchy dried egg noodles and are sold in 3 and 6-ounce cellophane bags.

4 cups (1¼lb) savoy cabbage, shredded
4 green onions, chopped finely
2 stalks celery, sliced finely
7-10 red globe radishes, sliced finely
1 medium carrot, sliced finely
2oz snow pea sprouts
1½ tablespoons sesame seeds, toasted
7oz fried noodles
½ cup peanut oil
3 tablespoons cider vinegar
¼ cup firmly packed brown sugar
2 teaspoons soy sauce
½ teaspoon sesame oil
1 clove garlic, crushed

Just before serving, gently toss cabbage, onions, celery, radishes, carrot, sprouts, seeds, noodles and combined remaining ingredients in large bowl.

SERVES 6 TO 8

Best made just before serving

CHAR-GRILLED CHILI SQUID WITH RIBBON VEGETABLES

The fresh Hokkien mee you buy packaged at the supermarket needs no pre-cooking; just rinse under or submerge in hot water to help separate and loosen the strands.

2lb squid, cleaned, tentacles removed
3 tablespoons lime juice
1 teaspoon fish sauce
½ cup sweet chili sauce
3 tablespoons chopped fresh cilantro
1lb Hokkien mee
1 medium carrot
1 medium green zucchini
1 medium yellow zucchini
1 medium sweet red bell pepper
1½ tablespoons white vinegar
3 tablespoons lime juice, extra
1 teaspoon sugar
½ cup olive oil
1½ tablespoons chopped fresh cilantro, extra

Cut squid in half lengthwise; make shallow scores in criss-cross pattern on inside surface, cut into 1-inch pieces. Mix squid with combined juice, sauces and cilantro in large bowl. Cover; refrigerate 3 hours or overnight.

Rinse noodles under hot water; drain. Transfer to large bowl; separate noodles with a fork.

Drain squid; discard marinade. Cook squid, in batches, on heated oiled griddle until just cooked and curled.

Using a vegetable peeler, finely slice carrot and both zucchini into paper-thin ribbons. Quarter pepper; remove and discard seeds and membranes. Using a sharp knife, cut pepper into extremely thin strips.

Just before serving, gently toss the cooled squid, noodles and vegetable ribbons in large bowl with combined remaining ingredients.

SERVES 4 TO 6

Squid best prepared 1 day ahead

Storage Covered, in refrigerator

Opposite above Sweet chili prawn salad
Opposite Crunchy coleslaw with fried noodles
Above Char-grilled chili squid with ribbon vegetables

FRESH CRAB AND SMOKED SALMON SPRINGTIME SALAD

Bean thread noodles must only be soaked long enough to just soften them: too long and they become stodgy and can break up.

4oz bean thread noodles
8oz asparagus
7oz snow peas, thinly sliced
3¹/₂ oz sliced smoked salmon
8oz shredded fresh crab meat
1 small cucumber, thinly sliced
4 green onions, sliced finely
¹/₂ cup olive oil
¹/₄ cup lemon juice
1 teaspoon finely grated lemon rind
1 clove garlic, crushed finely
1 teaspoon Dijon mustard
2 teaspoons finely chopped fresh dill

Place noodles in medium heatproof bowl, cover with boiling salted water, let stand only until just tender; drain.

Snap off and discard tough ends of asparagus; cut spears in half. Boil, steam or microwave asparagus and snow peas, separately, until just tender; drain. Rinse under cold water; drain.

Separate salmon slices; cut into ¹/₂-inch strips. Gently toss noodles, asparagus, snow peas, salmon, crab, cucumber and onions in large bowl with combined remaining ingredients.

SERVES 4 TO 6

Best made just before serving

PEKING DUCK SALAD

The delicate pancakes traditionally served with the first course of a Peking duck banquet are replaced by fine, fresh egg noodles in this main-course salad.

4 (2lb) boneless duck breasts
1/3 cup hoisin sauce
8oz fresh egg noodles
1 small cucumber, seeded, cut into 1/4-inch slices
2 green onions, sliced
3oz snow pea sprouts
3 tablespoons hoisin sauce, extra
1 1/2 tablespoons plum sauce
3 tablespoons rice vinegar
1/4 cup peanut oil

Place duck in large baking dish; brush with hoisin sauce. Bake, uncovered, at 350°F about 45 minutes or until cooked. Remove from pan; discard fat. When cool, cut into 1/4-inch slices.

Cook noodles in large pan of boiling salted water, uncovered, until just tender; drain. Rinse under cold water; drain.

Just before serving, gently toss duck and noodles in large bowl with cucumber, onions, bean sprouts and combined remaining ingredients.

SERVES 4 TO 6

Peking duck salad best made just before serving. Duck breasts can be baked 1 day ahead

Storage Covered, in refrigerator
Freeze Duck breasts suitable

◰ **WE HAVE TRIED** to be as specific as possible when it came to describing the noodle used in each recipe. However, if you can't find the specific noodle called for in the recipe, it's fine to substitute a variety which requires similar preparation and approximately the same cooking time. As long as you stay within the same basic ingredient family — wheat flour, rice flour, etc — and use a dried or fresh variety as called for, you're on the right track to success.

Meat with the works

◰ In keeping with the health-conscious mood of our times we've learned the value of quality rather than quantity and adjusted our butcher's orders accordingly. We've also tempered some of our favorite recipes by adding that other completely soul-nourishing staple – noodles.
Here, lamb, beef, pork and veal star in a globetrotting array of dishes.

BEEF WITH SUN-DRIED TOMATO SAUCE

Any thin fresh noodle will work well with this lusciously rich sauce.

8 sun-dried tomatoes in oil, undrained
3 tablespoons balsamic vinegar
1¹/₂lb whole piece beef rib eye steak or filet mignon
¹/₄ cup butter, softened
1 clove garlic, crushed
¹/₂ teaspoon sambal oelek
12oz fresh egg noodles
3 tablespoons shredded fresh basil

Drain tomatoes over small measuring cup; reserve oil. (Add enough olive oil to make ¹/₄ cup.) Finely chop tomatoes.

Combine oil and vinegar in jar; shake vinaigrette well.

Coat piece of beef with 3 tablespoons of the vinaigrette in large bowl. Cook beef on heated oiled griddle (or grill or barbecue) until browned all over and cooked as desired. Remove beef, cover; let stand 10 minutes. Slice beef thinly; cover to keep warm.

Combine butter, garlic, sambal oelek and half the tomatoes in small bowl.

Just before serving, cook noodles in large pan of salted boiling water, uncovered, until just tender; drain.

Gently toss hot noodles and basil in large bowl with butter mixture until butter is melted. Top noodle mixture with beef. Sprinkle with remaining tomatoes; drizzle with remaining vinaigrette.

SERVES 4 TO 6

Best made just before serving

PORK AND VEAL KOFTA

Soak bamboo skewers in water for 1 hour to prevent them from scorching. If fresh chow mein noodles are unavailable, try using an extremely thin fresh egg noodle instead.

1lb ground pork
1lb ground veal
1¹/₂ tablespoons ground cumin
2 cloves garlic, crushed
1 small onion, chopped finely
¹/₄ cup finely chopped
    dried apricots
1¹/₂ tablespoons fresh cilantro
¹/₄ cup slivered almonds,
    toasted, chopped
1 teaspoon hot paprika
6oz fresh chow mein, chopped
1 egg, beaten
³/₄ cup yogurt
1¹/₂ tablespoons fresh mint,
    chopped
1 teaspoon ground cumin, extra
1 teaspoon sugar

Combine ground meats, cumin, garlic, onion, apricots, cilantro, almonds, paprika, noodles and egg in large bowl. Cover; refrigerate 30 minutes. Roll rounded tablespoons of mixture into oval-shaped kofta; thread 3 kofta onto each skewer.

Cook kofta, in batches, on heated oiled griddle (or grill or barbecue), until browned and cooked through. Serve kofta with Yogurt Sauce.

Yogurt Sauce Combine yogurt, mint, extra cumin and sugar in small bowl.

SERVES 4 TO 6
Kofta and yogurt sauce can be prepared 1 day ahead

Storage Covered, separately, in refrigerator
Freeze Kofta suitable

◰ **WHILE IT'S** fine to make substitutions when cooking with noodles, read the contents' description on the package to make sure you're substituting a similar kind of noodle. Some labels can be very misleading; for example, some noodles described as egg don't contain any but are simply an egg-yolk yellow in color; another package might be called fresh egg, when in fact, it's a dried noodle to which a "fresh egg" was added during the manufacturing process.

Above left Pork and veal kofta
Left Mustard-curry pork slices in mushroom sauce
Opposite Lamb with garlic noodles

LAMB WITH GARLIC NOODLES

We used Japanese udon here and suggest you do, too, if this wholesome wheat noodle is available in your area. You will use 1/3 cup of garlic mayonnaise here; store the remainder in a tightly sealed jar, the surface covered with a little olive oil, in refrigerator for 1 day and use it in a dressing for a green salad.

1lb boneless lamb tenderloin
2 teaspoons cracked black pepper
1¹/₂ tablespoons finely grated lemon rind
¹/₂ cup olive oil
8oz udon
1¹/₂ tablespoons cider vinegar
8oz cherry tomatoes, halved
¹/₄ cup fresh basil
vegetable oil, for deep-frying
1 large onion, sliced thinly

GARLIC MAYONNAISE
1 medium bulb garlic, peeled, chopped coarsely
1 egg yolk
2 teaspoons water
3 tablespoons lemon juice
1 cup olive oil

Combine lamb tenderloin, pepper, rind and 2 tablespoons of the olive oil in a large bowl. Cover lamb; refrigerate 3 hours or overnight.

Cook lamb on heated oiled griddle (or grill or barbecue) until browned all over and cooked as desired. Remove lamb, cover; let stand 10 minutes. Slice lamb thinly; cover to keep warm.

Cook noodles in large pan of boiling salted water, uncovered, until just tender; drain.

Combine remaining olive oil, vinegar and 1 teaspoon of the Garlic Mayonnaise in jar; shake vinaigrette well. Gently toss lamb, noodles, tomatoes and basil with vinaigrette in large bowl.

Heat vegetable oil in large pan; deep-fry onion rings, in batches, until browned and crisp. Drain onion rings on paper towels. Top noodles and lamb with onion rings and the remainder of the ¹/₃ cup of the Garlic Mayonnaise.

Garlic Mayonnaise Blend or process garlic, egg yolk, water and juice until combined. With motor operating, gradually pour in oil; process until thick.

SERVES 4

Lamb with garlic noodles best made just before serving. Lamb and garlic mayonnaise can be prepared 1 day ahead

Storage Covered, separately, in refrigerator

MUSTARD-CURRY PORK SLICES IN MUSHROOM SAUCE

Any dried noodle can be used here but we liked it best with these flat dried wheat noodles.

2 teaspoons mild curry powder
1¹/₂ tablespoons stone ground mustard
2 (1lb) boneless pork chops
1¹/₂ tablespoons olive oil
1 large onion, sliced
1 clove garlic, crushed
8oz button mushrooms, sliced
¹/₄ cup dry white wine
3 tablespoons Dijon mustard
1 cup cream
¹/₄ cup water
8oz dried wheat noodles
1¹/₂ tablespoons chopped fresh parsley

Spread combined curry powder and stone ground mustard over pork; place in greased baking dish. Bake, uncovered, in 350°F oven about 30 minutes or until cooked as desired. Remove pork, cover; let let stand 10 minutes. Slice pork thinly; cover to keep warm.

Heat oil in medium pan; cook onion and garlic, stirring, until onion is soft. Add mushrooms; cook, stirring, until just tender. Stir in wine. Bring to boil; simmer until almost all liquid evaporates. Stir in Dijon mustard with cream and water; cook, stirring, until hot.

Meanwhile, cook noodles in large pan of boiling water, uncovered, until just tender; drain.

Gently toss noodles with pork and mushroom sauce in large bowl; sprinkle with parsley.

SERVES 4 TO 6

Best made just before serving

SUKIYAKI

Perhaps Japan's most well-known dish, sukiyaki (pronounced SKEE-YÁH-KEE) is easy to make at home – and it makes a fabulous dinner party main course: simply double the quantities below to feed 8 people. While a traditional sukiyaki pan can be purchased from Japanese or Asian kitchen shops, your electric skillet is a good substitute for table-top cooking. Only a small quantity of sukiyaki is cooked at a time to ensure the vegetables are not overdone. Each guest has their own bowl which, traditionally, has a broken raw egg in it: the first spoonful of hot sukiyaki cooks the egg.

8 dried shiitake mushrooms
2 green onions, sliced diagonally
  into 2-inch pieces
1 small green bell pepper,
  seeded, sliced
1/4 small Chinese (napa)
  cabbage, chopped
1lb spinach, trimmed
5oz bean sprouts
3oz shirataki noodles
1lb whole piece beef rib eye steak,
  or filet mignon sliced thinly
10oz block firm tofu, drained
  and cubed
3 tablespoons peanut oil
4 eggs
  MIRIN SAUCE
1/2 cup light soy sauce
1/2 cup water
1/4 cup dark soy sauce
1/4 cup mirin
1/4 cup sugar
1 teaspoon dashi granules

Place mushrooms in small heatproof bowl, cover with boiling water, let stand 20 minutes; drain. Discard stems; slice caps. Arrange vegetables, sprouts, noodles, beef and tofu on platter.

In a sukiyaki pan (or electric skillet) at the table, heat 2 teaspoons of the oil; stir-fry a quarter of the beef and onions until just cooked. Add a quarter of the mushrooms, peppers, cabbage, spinach, noodles and tofu to pan; stir-fry until just cooked. Add a quarter of the sprouts and Mirin Sauce; cook 30 seconds. Serve immediately in individual bowls. Repeat with remaining ingredients.

Mirin Sauce Stir all ingredients in medium pan over low heat until sugar dissolves; simmer gently 10 minutes.

SERVES 4

Sukiyaki ingredients can be prepared 3 hours ahead. Mirin sauce can be made 1 day ahead

Storage Covered, separately, in refrigerator

LAMB WITH ROASTED TOMATOES AND WALNUTS

You can use any fresh noodles you like in this recipe since they're not cooked with the meat; here we used Hokkien mee.

1 1/2lb whole pieces
  lamb tenderloin
3 tablespoons balsamic vinegar
3 tablespoons lemon juice
1/4 cup olive oil
1 1/2 tablespoons chopped
  fresh rosemary
2 teaspoons brown sugar
8 medium plum tomatoes,
  quartered lengthwise
1 teaspoon salt
1 teaspoon cracked black pepper
1 small whole garlic bulb
1 1/4lb Hokkien mee
4oz baby spinach leaves
3/4 cup walnuts, toasted

Combine lamb, vinegar, lemon juice, oil, rosemary and sugar in large bowl. Cover; refrigerate 3 hours or overnight.

Place tomatoes, cut-side up, on wire rack over baking dish; sprinkle with salt and pepper. Wrap garlic in foil, place on rack with tomatoes. Bake, uncovered, in 350°F oven about 1 hour or until tomatoes and garlic are very soft. When cool enough to handle, peel garlic; reserve pulp.

Drain lamb over large bowl; reserve marinade. Cook lamb on heated oiled griddle (or grill or barbecue) until browned both sides and cooked as desired. Remove lamb, cover; let stand 10 minutes. Slice lamb thinly; cover to keep warm.

Rinse noodles under hot water; drain. Transfer to large bowl; separate noodles with a fork.

Place reserved marinade in small pan; boil 1 minute. Stir in garlic pulp.

Gently toss hot noodles with spinach, walnuts, lamb and hot marinade in large bowl. Add tomatoes; toss gently.

SERVES 4 TO 6

Lamb with roasted tomatoes and walnuts must be made just before serving. Lamb best marinated 1 day ahead

Storage Covered, in refrigerator

◧ **SHIRATAKI** The translation of the Japanese name as "white waterfall" rather romantically describes these transparent thin noodles which are sold both dried and fresh in water packs. They are made from a root vegetable called konnyaku, meaning "devil's tongue" which is also how they are sometimes labeled. Dried shirataki need to be softened by soaking in hot water for a few minutes before adding to dishes such as sukiyaki. Bean thread noodles could be substituted if shirataki are unavailable.

Opposite Sukiyaki
Above Lamb with roasted tomatoes and walnuts

CHINESE ROAST PORK WITH STACKED NOODLE OMELETTES

This impressive dish uses mung bean thread noodles in the omelettes but you can substitute a fine fresh egg noodle if you like – but remember to alter the noodles' cooking time accordingly.

1/4 cup light soy sauce
3 tablespoons black bean sauce
1 clove garlic, crushed
2 teaspoons grated fresh ginger
3 (1¹/₂lb) boneless pork chops
4oz bean thread noodles
10 eggs, beaten
3 green onions, sliced thinly
3 tablespoons peanut oil

BLACK BEAN SAUCE
3 teaspoons cornstarch
1 cup chicken stock
1/4 cup black bean sauce
1/4 teaspoon sesame oil

Spread combined sauces, garlic and ginger over pork in shallow dish. Cover; refrigerate 3 hours or overnight. Remove pork from marinade; discard marinade.

Place pork on wire rack in baking dish; bake, uncovered, at 350°F for 30 minutes or until pork is cooked as desired, brushing occasionally with pan juices. Remove pork from oven, cover; let stand 10 minutes. Slice pork thinly; cover to keep warm.

Place noodles in medium heatproof bowl, cover with boiling water, let stand until just tender; drain. Cut noodles into small pieces over large bowl; whisk in eggs and onion.

Brush 8-inch heavy-based pan with some of the peanut oil; heat pan. Pour in 1/4 cup omelette mixture; cook, uncovered, until set underneath. Turn, cook other side. Place omelette on sheet of parchment. Repeat with remaining oil and omelette mixture, layering cooked omelettes between separate pieces of parchment. You need 12 omelettes.

Place 1 omelette on each of 4 serving plates, top with some of the pork, then another omelette and more pork, topping each stack with a third omelette. Drizzle with Black Bean Sauce before serving.

Black Bean Sauce Blend cornstarch with a little stock in small pan; gradually stir in remaining stock, sauce and oil. Stir over heat until mixture boils and thickens.

SERVES 4

Omelettes best made just before serving. Pork can be marinated 1 day ahead. Black bean sauce can be made 1 day ahead

Storage Covered, separately, in refrigerator

SINGAPORE NOODLES

This combination of pork, prawns and thin fresh egg noodles will help conjure visions of a meal in a Singaporean night market.

10 dried shiitake mushrooms
1lb fresh egg noodles
3 tablespoons peanut oil
5 cloves garlic, crushed
1¹/₂ tablespoons grated fresh ginger
3 tablespoons curry paste
8oz can water chestnuts, drained, chopped
4 green onions, chopped
8oz Chinese barbecue pork, sliced
1lb medium uncooked prawns, shelled, deveined
3 tablespoons light soy sauce
3 tablespoons oyster sauce
3 tablespoons dry sherry
3 eggs, beaten
2 teaspoons sesame oil

Place mushrooms in small heatproof bowl, cover with boiling water, let stand 20 minutes; drain. Discard stems; chop caps finely.

Rinse noodles under cold water; drain.

Heat peanut oil in wok or large pan; stir-fry garlic, ginger and paste about 2 minutes or until fragrant. Add mushrooms, chestnuts, onion and pork; stir-fry about 2 minutes or until chestnuts are browned lightly. Add prawns; stir-fry until prawns change color. Add noodles and combined sauces and sherry; stir-fry until most of the liquid is absorbed. Add combined eggs and sesame oil; stir-fry until eggs are just cooked.

SERVES 4

Must be made just before serving

Above Singapore noodles
Opposite Chinese roast pork with stacked noodle omelettes

LAMB CHOPS WITH THYME-TOASTED NOODLES

We used a thin fresh Chinese egg noodle here which nicely complemented the toasted breadcrumbs.

1/3 cup olive oil
4 cups fresh breadcrumbs
2 cloves garlic, crushed
2 teaspoons chopped fresh thyme
12 (1 3/4lb) lamb rib chops
5oz button mushrooms,
 sliced thinly
1 cup dry red wine
3/4 cup water
3/4 cup beef stock
2 tablespoons Dijon mustard
1 1/2 tablespoons tomato paste
1lb fresh egg noodles

Heat 1/4 cup of the oil in large pan; cook breadcrumbs, garlic and thyme, stirring, 15 minutes or until golden and crisp. Place breadcrumbs in large bowl.

Heat remaining oil in same pan; cook chops, in batches, until browned both sides and cooked as desired. Cover to keep warm. Add mushrooms to same pan; cook, stirring, until just soft. Add combined wine, water, stock, mustard and paste. Bring to boil; simmer, uncovered, about 10 minutes or until reduced by half, stirring occasionally.

Meanwhile, cook noodles in large pan of salted boiling water, uncovered, until just tender; drain. Gently toss noodles with toasted breadcrumbs in large bowl. Divide noodles among serving plates; top with lamb chops; spoon sauce over top.

SERVES 4

Best made on day of serving

◻ **SLIP, SLOP, SLURP** Throughout Asia, lusty slurping of noodles is regarded more as a compliment to the cook than bad manners. In Japan, for instance, participants in Zen retreats are only allowed to break their silence when they eat noodles as it is believed impossible to eat them quietly.

Opposite Lamb chops with thyme-toasted noodles
Above Satay beef noodles

SATAY BEEF NOODLES

Fresh chow mein are becoming easier to obtain, with large supermarket chains stocking them these days. Substitute Hokkien mee, however, if you can't find fresh chow mein.

3 tablespoons peanut oil
1¹/₂lb beef round steak, sliced thinly
1 medium onion, sliced
1 clove garlic, crushed
¹/₂ cup smooth peanut butter
¹/₄ cup sweet chili sauce
²/₃ cup coconut milk
³/₄ cup chicken stock
3 tablespoons lime juice
1 teaspoon sugar
1¹/₂ tablespoons chopped fresh cilantro

1lb fresh chow mein
2oz garlic chives, halved lengthwise

Heat half the oil in wok or large pan; stir-fry beef, in batches, until browned and almost cooked. Cover to keep warm.

Heat remaining oil in same pan; stir-fry onion and garlic until onion is soft. Add peanut butter, chili sauce, milk, stock, lime juice, sugar and cilantro; stir-fry until hot.

Meanwhile, rinse chow mein in hot water to separate; drain.

Return beef and any juices to pan. Gently toss chives and noodles with beef; stir-fry until just hot.

SERVES 4

Best made just before serving

ROASTED SWEET RED BELL PEPPERS FILLED WITH PORK AND VEAL

Many Chinese dried wheat noodles have various vegetables added to the dough before they are extruded – although it's the vegetable's color that dominates, not the taste. We used spinach-flavored thin wheat noodles here but you can substitute them with the color of your choice.

5oz dried wheat noodles
1¹/₂ tablespoons olive oil
1 medium onion, chopped
2 cloves garlic, crushed
2 small fresh red chilis, seeded, chopped finely
8oz ground pork
8oz ground veal
14oz can tomatoes
3oz (4-5) cherry tomatoes, quartered
2oz baby spinach leaves
1¹/₂ tablespoons chopped fresh oregano

BEEF, RAMEN AND BOK CHOY STIR-FRY

Ramen can be dressed up in dishes like this so that it no longer resembles the 2-minute variety we all have in our kitchens.

3 tablespoons peanut oil
1lb lean beef strips
1 large red onion, sliced
1¹/₂ tablespoons grated fresh ginger
2 cloves garlic, crushed
1 large red bell pepper, sliced
1¹/₄lb baby bok choy, trimmed, sliced
8oz ramen
3 tablespoons oyster sauce
1¹/₂ tablespoons sweet chili sauce
1¹/₂ tablespoons black bean sauce
1¹/₂ tablespoons soy sauce
2 teaspoons rice vinegar

Heat oil in wok or large pan; stir-fry beef, in batches, until browned and cooked as desired. Add onion, ginger, garlic and peppers to same pan; stir-fry 2 minutes or until onion is almost soft. Add bok choy; stir-fry 1 minute.

Meanwhile, cook noodles in large pan of boiling salted water, uncovered, until just tender; drain. Place in large bowl; separate noodles with fork.

Return beef to pan; gently toss with noodles and combined sauces and vinegar. Stir-fry 2 minutes or until hot.

SERVES 6

Best made just before serving

2 medium sweet red bell peppers
2 medium green bell peppers
2 medium yellow bell peppers

Cook noodles in large pan of boiling salted water, uncovered, until just tender; drain.

Heat oil in large pan; cook onion, garlic and chili, stirring, until onion is soft. Add ground meats; cook, stirring, until browned. Add undrained crushed tomatoes. Bring to boil; simmer 10 minutes or until mixture thickens slightly. Add cherry tomatoes and spinach; cook, stirring, until spinach is just wilted. Remove from heat; stir in oregano and noodles.

Cut off and reserve tops of bell peppers; remove and discard seeds and membranes from all peppers. Place peppers in oiled baking dish; fill with noodle mixture, replace tops. Bake, uncovered, at 350°F about 45 minutes or until peppers are tender and browned lightly.

SERVES 4 TO 6

Can be prepared 3 hours ahead

Storage   Covered, in refrigerator

BEEF STROGANOFF WITH A TRIO OF MUSHROOMS

Triple the mushrooms and incorporate the noodles for this new-look stroganoff.

8oz dried egg noodles
3 tablespoons olive oil
1lb whole piece beef filet mignon, cut into thin strips
2 large onions, sliced
2 cloves garlic, crushed
5oz oyster mushrooms, sliced
5oz brown mushrooms, sliced
5oz shimeji mushrooms, trimmed
1¹/₂ tablespoons tomato paste
1¹/₂ tablespoons Worcestershire sauce
2 teaspoons sweet paprika
1¹/₄ cups sour cream
1 cup beef stock
2 teaspoons lemon juice

Cook noodles in large pan of boiling salted water, uncovered, until just tender; drain. Rinse under cold water; drain.

Heat half of the oil in large pan; cook beef, in batches, until browned.

Heat remaining oil in same pan; cook onions and garlic, stirring, until onions are soft. Add mushrooms; cook, stirring, 2 minutes. Return beef to pan with combined paste, sauce, paprika, cream, stock and lemon juice. Bring to boil; simmer 10 minutes. Gently toss noodles with beef mixture in pan until hot.

SERVES 4 TO 6

Best made just before serving

Opposite   Beef, ramen and bok choy stir-fry
Left   Roasted sweet red bell peppers filled with pork and veal
Above   Beef stroganoff with a trio of mushrooms

TERIYAKI BEEF WITH SOMEN

Any thin, round wheat noodle can be used with teriyaki beef but somen makes it more authentically Japanese.

1/4 cup peanut oil
**1 1/2lb whole piece beef filet
    mignon, sliced thinly**
1 large onion, sliced
2 cloves garlic, crushed
2 teaspoons grated fresh ginger
6oz somen
1/4 cup teriyaki sauce
1 1/2 tablespoon light soy sauce
3 tablespoons mirin
6 green onions, chopped

Heat 2 tablespoons of the oil in wok or large pan; stir-fry beef, in batches, until browned. Heat remaining oil in same pan; stir-fry onion, garlic and ginger 2 minutes.

Meanwhile, cook noodles in large pan of boiling salted water, uncovered, 1 minute only; drain. Rinse under cold water; drain.

Add combined sauces and mirin with green onion; stir-fry until mixture is hot. Return beef to pan with noodles; stir-fry 2 minutes or until noodles are hot.

SERVES 4

Best made just before serving

VEAL AND GREEN
BEAN MADRAS

We used veal shoulder, trimmed of all fat, in this recipe. We used dried wide flat wheat noodles from Taiwan which can be hard to find, but any dried flat wheat noodle will suit just fine.

3 tablespoons peanut oil
1 1/4lb diced veal shoulder
1 medium onion, chopped
2 cloves garlic, crushed
**3 tablespoons finely chopped or
    ground fresh lemon grass**
**3 tablespoons finely chopped
    fresh ginger**
1 teaspoon Madras curry powder
1 teaspoon ground turmeric
1 cup beef stock
1 cup coconut milk
1 teaspoon brown sugar
5oz green beans, sliced
6oz dried wheat noodles

Heat oil in large pan; cook veal, in batches, until browned. Add onion, garlic, lemon grass, ginger, curry powder and turmeric to same pan; cook, stirring, until onion is soft. Return veal to pan with combined stock, milk and sugar. Bring to boil; simmer, covered, 1 hour or until veal is tender. Add beans; simmer, uncovered, until beans are tender.

Just before serving, cook noodles in large pan of boiling salted water, uncovered, until just tender; drain. Stir noodles gently into veal mixture.

SERVES 4

Best made just before serving

▄ **SOMEN** This extremely thin wheat noodle from Japan is labeled somen if it is eggless, tamago somen if it contains egg. Usually sold dried in bundles held together by a paper band, somen makes a refreshing summer dish when served chilled with ice cubes. Take extreme care not to overcook somen as it can quickly become mushy.

Opposite Teriyaki beef with somen
Below Veal and green bean madras

SWEET-SOUR BEEF
IN NOODLE BASKETS

It's important to use fresh noodles for this recipe so that you have the flexibility required to shape the baskets. To make the noodle baskets you will need to use 2 wire strainers, the kind available from kitchenware stores – make sure they are completely made of metal... handles and all.

1lb whole piece beef filet mignon
1¹/₂ tablespoons plum sauce
1 teaspoon balsamic vinegar
3 tablespoons cracked black pepper
5oz cherry tomatoes, halved
2 teaspoons olive oil
1 medium yellow zucchini, sliced
1 medium eggplant, sliced
**   lengthwise**
2oz arugula, trimmed

GARLIC DRESSING
3 tablespoons olive oil
3 tablespoons balsamic vinegar
1 clove garlic, crushed
NOODLE BASKETS
6oz fresh egg noodles
vegetable oil, for deep-frying

Brush beef with combined sauce, vinegar and pepper. Cover; refrigerate 3 hours or overnight. Place beef on rack in baking dish. Toss tomatoes with oil in small bowl; place on rack with beef. Bake, uncovered, at 350°F 30 minutes or until beef is cooked as desired. Remove beef, cover; let stand 10 minutes. Slice beef thinly; cover to keep warm.

Cook zucchini and eggplant on heated oiled griddle (or grill or barbecue) until browned and just tender. Tear half the arugula into pieces. Gently toss beef, tomatoes, zucchini, eggplant, torn arugula and half the Garlic Dressing in large bowl.

Divide remaining arugula among serving plates, place Noodle Baskets on

arugula. Divide beef mixture among Noodle Baskets, drizzle with remaining Garlic Dressing.

Garlic Dressing Combine all ingredients in jar; shake well.

Noodle Baskets Divide noodles into 6 portions. Brush inside of 5-inch wire strainer with oil; line with 1 portion of the noodles. Oil underside of 4-inch strainer; press smaller strainer down firmly onto noodles. Heat oil in large pan; holding both handles together with an oven mitt, gently lower strainer baskets into hot oil. Deep-fry until noodles are golden brown and crisp; drain on paper towels. Repeat with remaining noodles.

SERVES 6

Noodle baskets can be made 1 day ahead

Storage In airtight container

Above Sweet-sour beef in noodle baskets
Opposite above Hokkien mee
Opposite Below Orange ginger lamb with crispy noodle triangles

HOKKIEN MEE

There are probably as many versions of Hokkien mee as there are of spaghetti bolognese. Hokkien mee can be found in the refrigerated section of many supermarkets. Thick teriyaki sauce may be substituted for ketjap manis, if unavailable.

1¹/4lb Hokkien mee
2 eggs, beaten
1¹/2 tablespoon water
¹/4 cup vegetable oil
3 tablespoons grated fresh ginger
4 cloves garlic, crushed
4 small fresh red chilis,
   seeded, chopped
2 teaspoons sugar
1 large sweet red bell pepper,
   seeded, sliced
1 small green bell pepper,
   seeded, sliced
4 green onions, sliced
2 cups shredded Chinese
   (napa) cabbage
1lb Chinese barbecue pork, sliced
¹/3 cup ketjap manis (or thick
   teriyaki sauce)
¹/4 cup oyster sauce

Rinse noodles under hot water; drain. Transfer to large bowl; separate noodles with a fork.

Heat large oiled non-stick pan; pour in half the combined eggs and water. Swirl pan to make a thin omelette; cook until just set. Transfer omelette to board, roll tightly; cut into thin strips. Repeat with remaining egg mixture.

Heat 1 tablespoon of the oil in wok or large pan; stir-fry ginger, garlic, chili and sugar until fragrant. Add vegetables; stir-fry until cabbage is just wilted. Remove vegetables from pan. Heat remaining oil in same pan; stir-fry noodles 2 minutes. Add vegetables, pork and combined sauces; stir-fry until hot. Serve sprinkled with omelette strips.

SERVES 4 TO 6

Best made just before serving

ORANGE GINGER LAMB WITH CRISPY NOODLE TRIANGLES

This noodle version of rosti is great to serve with many dishes as a crunchy surprise – even the kids will love them.

¹/2 cup orange juice
2 teaspoons grated fresh ginger
2 cloves garlic, crushed
1¹/2 tablespoons thick
   teriyaki sauce
1¹/2 tablespoons sweet chili sauce
3 tablespoons honey
12 (1³/4lb) lamb rib chops

CRISPY NOODLE TRIANGLES
12oz fresh egg noodles
¹/4 cup peanut oil

Combine orange juice, ginger, garlic, sauces and honey in large bowl; add chops, turn to coat in marinade. Cover; refrigerate 3 hours or overnight.

Drain chops; reserve marinade in same bowl. Cook chops in batches, in large heated oiled pan until browned both sides and cooked as desired, brushing with reserved marinade. Serve chops on Crispy Noodle Triangles.

Crispy Noodle Triangles Cook noodles in large pan of boiling salted water, uncovered, until just tender; drain. When cool, press noodles into 9 x 12 baking pan; refrigerate, 3 hours or overnight.

Turn noodle cake onto board; cut noodle cake in half lengthwise. Cut each half into 3 pieces crosswise; cut each piece diagonally in half to make 12 triangles. Heat oil in large pan; cook triangles, in batches, until browned and crisp. Drain triangles on paper towels.

SERVES 4

Lamb and noodle triangles can be prepared 1 day ahead

Storage Covered, separately, in refrigerator

MEE GORENG

This much-loved dish that translates simply as fried noodles, uses Peking noodles. You may substitute thick teriyaki sauce for ketjap manis, if unavailable.

1lb fresh wheat noodles
vegetable oil, for deep-frying
1 small onion, sliced
3 tablespoons raw peanuts
3 tablespoons peanut oil
1lb boneless pork chops,
    sliced thinly
5 cloves garlic, crushed
3 tablespoons grated fresh ginger
3 small fresh red chilis,
    seeded, chopped
10 fresh water chestnuts, sliced
18 long beans, sliced
2 stalks celery, chopped
2 baby bok choy, chopped
2 green onions, chopped
1/3 cup ketjap manis
3 tablespoons sweet chili sauce
1 1/2 tablespoons tamarind
    concentrate
1/3 cup vegetable stock
1 teaspoon sesame oil

Cook noodles in large pan of boiling salted water, uncovered, until just tender; drain.

Heat vegetable oil in small pan; deep-fry onion until browned. Drain onion on paper towels. Deep-fry peanuts in same hot oil until browned lightly. Drain on paper towels. Blend or process onion and peanuts until chopped finely.

Heat half the peanut oil in wok or large pan; stir-fry pork until browned both sides and cooked as desired. Remove pork; cover to keep warm. Heat remaining peanut oil in same pan; stir-fry garlic, ginger and chili until fragrant. Add water chestnuts and vegetables; stir-fry 2 minutes. Return pork to pan with noodles, sauces, tamarind, stock and sesame oil; stir-fry until hot. Serve sprinkled with deep-fried onion and peanut mixture.

SERVES 4

Best made just before serving

Opposite Mee goreng
Right Crusty lamb chops with cilantro pesto

⊏ **CRISPY NOODLES** Many varieties of clear noodle – dried rice, bean thread, arrowroot, shirataki, harusame – will puff up into white fluffy shreds when deep-fried in hot oil. They can then be used as a garnish, a bed for other food to be served on or as an ingredient, as in the Thai dish, mee krob. Pre-boiled fresh and dried egg noodles can also be deep-fried to make serving nests or edible bowls.

CRUSTY LAMB CHOPS WITH CILANTRO PESTO

Thin rice stick noodles, when used, crushed, as a coating for lamb chops, add spectacular crunch to this dish.

2 cups firmly packed fresh
    cilantro
1/4 cup grated romano cheese
3 tablespoons pine nuts, toasted
1 1/2 tablespoon balsamic vinegar
1/2 cup olive oil
1 clove garlic, chopped
12 (1 3/4lb) lamb rib chops
10oz dried rice noodles
all-purpose flour
2 eggs, beaten
vegetable oil, for deep-frying

Blend or process cilantro, cheese, nuts, vinegar, olive oil and garlic until pureed. Combine lamb chops and 1/4 cup of the cilantro pesto in large bowl. Cover; refrigerate 3 hours or overnight.

Place remaining cilantro pesto in small bowl; cover surface with plastic wrap, refrigerate until ready to use.

Bake lamb chops in greased baking dish, at 450°F, 10 minutes; cool 5 minutes.

Place noodles in plastic bag; crush into small pieces.

Toss lamb chops in flour, dip in eggs; press into crushed noodles. Heat vegetable oil in large pan; deep-fry cutlets, in batches, until noodles are golden brown and puffed. Drain on paper towels. Stir remaining cilantro pesto in small pan over heat until warm; serve with lamb chops.

SERVES 4 TO 6

Marinated lamb and cilantro pesto can be made 1 day ahead

Storage Covered, separately, in refrigerator

BAKED BEEF 'N' NOODLES

This is one the whole family will love, the tasty combination of beef with plump, flavorful noodles will win you points every time.

1lb Hokkien mee
3 tablespoons olive oil
2lb beef chuck steak, cut into 1-inch cubes
1 large onion, sliced
4 cloves garlic, crushed
2 celery stalks, sliced
2 medium carrots, chopped
2 baby eggplants, sliced
1/4 cup dry red wine
1 1/2 cups beef stock
3 tablespoons tomato paste
14oz can tomato puree
1 cup fresh breadcrumbs
1 1/2 cups grated cheddar cheese
1 1/2 tablespoons chopped fresh parsley

Rinse noodles in hot water; drain. Transfer to large bowl; separate noodles with a fork.

Heat half the oil in large pan; cook beef, in batches, until browned. Heat remaining oil in same pan; cook onion and garlic, stirring, until onion is soft. Add celery, carrots and eggplants; cook, stirring 5 minutes or until vegetables are just tender. Return beef to pan with wine, stock, paste and puree. Bring to boil; simmer, covered, about 1 hour or until beef is tender. Stir noodles gently into beef mixture.

Transfer beef and noodle mixture to 10-cup ovenproof dish; sprinkle with combined remaining ingredients. Bake, uncovered, at 350°F about 25 minutes, or until browned.

SERVES 4 TO 6

Can be prepared 1 day ahead

Storage Covered, in refrigerator

◰ **FRESH WHEAT NOODLES** Commonly labelled Hokkien mee or stir-fry noodles, these round, thick, yellow-beige noodles are the base for many stir-fried dishes. They do not usually contain egg, though some cookbooks suggest they do. The noodles separate readily if they are rinsed in hot water before adding to the recipe.

LAMB SHANKS WITH BAKED NOODLES

We used fresh Peking noodles made from wheat flour but any fresh stir-fry noodle can be used instead.

3 tablespoons olive oil
8 (3 1/2lb) lamb shanks
1 medium onion, sliced
2 cloves garlic, crushed
2 14oz cans tomatoes
1/4 cup dry red wine
1/4 cup tomato paste
1 cup beef stock
4 sprigs fresh oregano
5oz button mushrooms, halved
10oz fresh wheat noodles

Heat oil in large flameproof dish; cook lamb, in batches, until browned all over. Cover lamb; reserve 1 1/2 tablespoons of dish juices, discard remainder.

Add onion and garlic to same dish; cook, stirring, until onion is soft. Return lamb to same dish with undrained crushed tomatoes, wine, paste, stock and oregano. Bake, uncovered, at 350°F for 1 1/2 hours. Remove lamb from dish; gently stir mushrooms and noodles into juices in dish. Return lamb to dish; gently mix in among noodles. Bake, uncovered, about 25 minutes, or until top is crisp.

SERVES 4 TO 6

Can be made 3 hours ahead

Storage Covered, in refrigerator

Opposite Baked beef 'n' noodles
Right Lamb shanks with baked noodles

STIR-FRIED UDON AND CRISPY LAMB

Here is an unusual treatment of classic Japanese udon that is sure to impress. Substitute any dried flat wheat noodle, if you wish.

1 clove garlic, crushed
1/2 cup hoisin sauce
1 1/2 tablespoons soy sauce
1 1/2 tablespoons sweet chili sauce
1 1/2 tablespoons oyster sauce
1 1/2lb whole piece lamb tenderloin, cut into thin strips
all-purpose flour
vegetable oil, for deep-frying
12oz udon
3 tablespoons water
1lb choy sum

Combine garlic and sauces in large bowl; reserve 3 tablespoons of marinade mixture in jar, refrigerate. Add lamb to bowl; coat with remaining marinade. Cover; refrigerate 3 hours or overnight.

Drain lamb; discard marinade. Roll lamb in flour; shake off excess. Heat oil in large pan; deep-fry lamb, in batches, until browned and crisp. Drain on paper towels. Cover to keep warm.

Cook noodles in large pan of boiling salted water, uncovered, until just tender; drain.

Boil combined reserved marinade and water in wok or large pan; stir-fry choy sum until just wilted. Remove choy sum mixture; cover to keep warm. Add noodles to pan; stir-fry until hot. Divide noodles among serving plates; top with choy sum, then crispy lamb.

SERVES 4

Lamb can be prepared 1 day ahead

Storage Covered, in refrigerator

Above Stir-fried udon and crispy lamb
Opposite Curried beef and lime noodles

CURRIED BEEF
AND LIME NOODLES

We used dried wide rice stick noodles here; an interesting alternative would be to use mung bean thread noodles. You need fine slices of sweet red bell peppers and green onions to make curls.

1 small sweet red bell pepper
1 small yellow bell pepper
4 green onions
8oz dried wide rice noodles
1^1/$_2$ tablespoons peanut oil
1^1/$_2$lb ground beef
1 medium onion, chopped
2 cloves garlic, crushed
2 kaffir lime leaves, torn
^{1}/$_3$ cup red curry paste
2 teaspoons white miso
3 tablespoons lime juice
3 tablespoons fish sauce
1^1/$_2$ cups beef stock
2 teaspoons cornstarch
3 tablespoons fresh cilantro

Quarter peppers; remove seeds. Place peppers, skin-side down, on cutting board. Cut peppers horizontally, removing membranes and some of the flesh until ^{1}/$_8$-inch thick; discard membranes and flesh. Slice peppers into ^{1}/$_8$-inch strips.

Halve green onions lengthwise; slice halves into ^{1}/$_8$-inch strips. Place peppers and onion in large bowl of iced water. Cover; refrigerate 1 hour or until pepper strips curl.

Place noodles in large heatproof bowl, cover with boiling water, let stand only until just tender; drain. Rinse well under cold water; drain.

Heat half the oil in wok or large pan; cook beef, in batches, until well browned. Cover to keep warm.

Heat remaining oil in same pan; stir-fry onion, garlic and lime leaves until onion is soft. Add combined paste, miso, juice and sauce; stir-fry 1 minute. Add blended stock and cornstarch. Bring to boil; simmer, stirring, until thickened slightly. Return beef to pan with noodles; stir-fry until hot. Serve topped with drained curled pepper and green onion strips, and cilantro.

SERVES 4 TO 6

Best made just before serving

◗ **UDON** Available fresh and dried, these Japanese broad white wheat noodles are similar to those found in chicken noodle soup. Particularly popular in southern Japan, udon built its reputation as a soup noodle, but is equally at home in stir-fries and hotpots.

Counting
your chickens

If there is a cooking equivalent of the meeting of like minds, it's the combination of chicken and noodles. Both ingredients bring an amazing versatility to the partnership: they absorb flavors brilliantly, lend themselves to a host of preparation techniques and can be teamed with an enormous array of vegetables, herbs and spices. This gathering of recipes celebrates a marriage made in culinary heaven.

CHILLED SOBA WITH FENNEL AND CHICKEN

The global village comes alive in this dish, where East meets West in a lavishly presented cold main course.

8oz soba
5 green onions
$^1/_3$ cup chicken stock
$^1/_3$ cup dry white wine
2-inch piece fresh ginger, sliced
4 (1$^1/_3$lb) boneless chicken breasts
1 medium bulb fennel, sliced thinly
1$^1/_2$ tablespoons sesame seeds, toasted
1$^1/_2$ tablespoons mirin
3 tablespoons seasoned rice vinegar
3 tablespoons light soy sauce
3 tablespoons peanut oil
1$^1/_2$ tablespoons lemon juice
$^1/_2$ teaspoon sesame oil

Cook noodles in large pan of boiling, salted water, uncovered, until just tender; drain. Cover; refrigerate 3 hours or overnight.

Chop white parts of onions; reserve green leaves. Combine white parts of onions, stock, wine and ginger in large pan. Bring to boil; simmer. Add chicken; poach, covered, about 10 minutes or until tender. Remove chicken; cut into $^1/_2$-inch slices. Strain stock mixture into large bowl, discard ginger and onion; return stock to same pan. Add fennel, bring to boil; simmer, stirring, until fennel is soft. Remove fennel; save stock for use as broth or for use in cooking rice or another noodle dish.

Thinly slice reserved green onion leaves. Gently toss with noodles, chicken, fennel and sesame seeds in large bowl with combined remaining ingredients.

SERVES 4 TO 6

Noodles and chicken can be prepared 1 day ahead

Storage Covered, separately, in refrigerator

LIME-ROASTED SPRING CHICKENS WITH NOODLES

The combination of mint, lime and cucumber makes a real treat for summertime feasting. We used wide rice stick noodles to complement the lightness of this recipe.

2 young chickens (1lb each), poussins, or cornish game hens
4 cloves garlic, crushed
2 teaspoons ground ginger
3 tablespoons finely grated lime rind
7oz dried rice noodles
1¹/₂ tablespoons butter, melted
2 burpless cucumbers
1 teaspoon cumin seeds, toasted, crushed
1 teaspoon yellow mustard seeds, toasted, crushed
¹/₂ teaspoon ground coriander
2 teaspoons sugar
3 tablespoons chopped fresh mint
¹/₂ cup lime juice
¹/₃ cup sweet chili sauce
1¹/₂ tablespoons finely chopped or ground fresh lemon grass
¹/₄ cup pine nuts, toasted

Cut along both sides of chickens' backbones; save backbones for use in making stock. Cut in half between breasts. Rinse under cold water; pat dry. Place chicken halves, skin-side up, in greased shallow baking dish. Combine garlic, ginger and rind in small bowl; press onto chicken. Cover; refrigerate 1 hour.

Place noodles in large heatproof bowl, cover with boiling water, let stand until just tender; drain.

Brush chicken with butter; bake, uncovered, in 450°F oven about 30 minutes, or until cooked.

Meanwhile, cut cucumbers in half crosswise; using a vegetable peeler, cut cucumber into ribbons. Combine cucumber ribbons and noodles in large bowl with seeds, ground coriander, sugar and mint.

Combine juice, sauce and lemon grass in jar; shake dressing well.

Divide noodle mixture among serving plates; top with chicken, drizzle with dressing, scatter with pine nuts.

SERVES 4

Chicken and dressing can be prepared 1 day ahead

Storage Covered, separately, in refrigerator

COMBINATION CHOW MEIN

Everyone's favorite in a Chinese restaurant is easily replicated at home with this simple recipe.

vegetable oil, for deep-frying
8oz dried chow mein
1lb medium uncooked prawns
3 tablespoons peanut oil
3 (1lb) boneless chicken
    breasts, diced
2 cloves garlic, crushed
1¹/₂ tablespoons grated
    fresh ginger
1 large sweet red bell pepper, sliced
1 8oz can water chestnuts,
    drained, sliced
6 green onions, sliced finely
8oz (1³/₄ cups) Chinese (napa)
    cabbage, shredded
3oz bean sprouts
¹/₃ cup chopped fresh garlic chives
¹/₄ cup light soy sauce
1¹/₂ tablespoons oyster sauce
¹/₂ teaspoon sesame oil
2 teaspoons cornstarch
¹/₂ cup chicken stock

Heat vegetable oil in large pan; deep-fry noodles, in batches, until puffed. Drain noodles on paper towels. Shell and devein prawns, leaving tails intact.

Heat half the peanut oil in wok or large pan; stir-fry chicken, in batches, until browned both sides and tender. Cover chicken to keep warm. Add prawns to same pan; stir-fry until prawns change color. Remove prawns; cover.

Heat remaining peanut oil in same pan; stir-fry garlic, ginger, pepper, water chestnuts and all but 1 rounded tablespoon of the onions until pepper is just tender.

Return chicken and prawns to pan; add cabbage, sprouts and chives, stir-fry until cabbage is just wilted. Stir in combined sauces, sesame oil and blended cornstarch and stock; stir-fry until mixture boils and thickens. Serve with deep-fried noodles; sprinkle with remaining onions.

SERVES 4 TO 6

Must be made just before serving

Opposite Lime-roasted spring chickens with noodles
Right Combination chow mein

BONELESS CHICKEN BREASTS WITH SOBA AND ARUGULA

The nutty flavor of these Japanese buckwheat noodles is enhanced by the piquancy of the peppercorns and arugula.

4 (1¹/₃lb) boneless chicken breasts
2 medium sweet red bell peppers
8oz soba
4oz arugula, trimmed
1 medium red onion, sliced

GREEN PEPPERCORN DRESSING
³/₄ cup light olive oil
¹/₄ cup white wine vinegar
1¹/₂ tablespoons green peppercorns, drained
1 clove garlic, peeled
1 teaspoon sugar

Cook chicken on heated oiled griddle (or grill or barbecue), brushing with ¹/₄ cup of the Green Peppercorn Dressing, until chicken is browned both sides and tender. Remove chicken; slice thinly.

Quarter peppers, remove seeds and membranes. Roast under broiler or in 500°F oven, skin-side up, until skin blisters and blackens. Wrap pepper pieces in plastic or paper, 5 minutes, peel away skin; cut peppers into 3-inch strips.

Cook noodles in large pan of boiling salted water, uncovered, until just tender; drain. Rinse under cold water; drain well.

Just before serving, gently toss chicken, peppers and noodles in large bowl with torn arugula, red onion and remaining Green Peppercorn Dressing.

Green Peppercorn Dressing Blend or process all ingredients until smooth.

SERVES 4 TO 6

Best made just before serving

PENANG STIR-FRY NOODLES AND CARAMELIZED CHICKEN

These spicy Asian flavors marry well with any fairly thin, dried wheat noodle.

1lb dried wheat noodles
3 tablespoons vegetable oil
4 (1¹/₃lb) boneless chicken breasts, sliced finely
5 cloves garlic, crushed
1¹/₂ tablespoons finely chopped fresh ginger
3 tablespoons finely chopped or ground fresh lemon grass
4 small fresh red chilis, seeded, chopped finely
¹/₃ cup brown sugar
3 tablespoons water
¹/₄ cup oyster sauce
3 tablespoons fish sauce
2 teaspoons tamarind concentrate
¹/₄ cup lime juice
¹/₄ cup fresh cilantro

Cook noodles in large pan of boiling, salted water, uncovered, until just tender; drain. Heat half the oil in wok or large pan; stir-fry chicken, in batches, until browned and tender. Cover to keep warm. Add remaining oil to same pan; stir-fry garlic, ginger, lemon grass and chili until fragrant. Stir in sugar and water; cook, stirring, until sugar caramelizes. Return chicken to pan; stir-fry until coated in caramelized sugar mixture. Stir in noodles with combined sauces, tamarind and lime juice. Simmer until sauce thickens slightly. Just before serving, sprinkle with cilantro.

SERVES 4

Best made just before serving

⌐ DRIED WHEAT NOODLES As the name suggests, these noodles are made of wheat flour. They may be colored with dyes or vegetable extracts and come in various guises ranging from the flat ho fen to tangled cakes labeled mein or "instant" noodles. They are equally at home in soups or stir-fries, in which case they have to be pre-cooked before adding to the wok.

Left Penang stir-fry noodles and caramelized chicken
Opposite Boneless chicken breasts with soba and arugula

RICE STICK-CRUSTED CHICKEN WITH GARLIC MASHED POTATOES

This crisp coating of whole dried rice stick noodles makes a great alternative to a traditional crumb coating.

3oz dried rice noodles
4 (1¹/₃lb) boneless chicken breasts
all-purpose flour
2 eggs, beaten
1 teaspoon hot paprika
1 teaspoon chicken base or bouillon cube
1 clove garlic, crushed
4 green onions, chopped finely
¹/₄ cup olive oil
5 medium potatoes, peeled, chopped
2 cloves garlic, crushed, extra
¹/₃ cup coarsely grated parmesan cheese
¹/₂ cup buttermilk
1¹/₂ tablespoons finely grated lemon rind
1¹/₂ tablespoons chopped fresh parsley

Place noodles in large heatproof bowl, cover with boiling water, let stand until just tender; drain.

Pound chicken breasts until uniform in thickness. Roll chicken in flour, then dip in egg; coat chicken with combined noodles, paprika, bouillon powder, garlic and onions.

Heat oil in large pan; cook chicken until browned both sides and tender. Remove chicken; cover to keep warm.

Meanwhile, boil, steam or microwave potatoes until tender; drain. Mash potatoes in large bowl with the extra garlic, cheese and buttermilk.

Sprinkle chicken with combined lemon rind and parsley; serve chicken with garlic mashed potatoes.

SERVES 4

Best made just before serving

Below Rice stick-crusted chicken with garlic mashed potatoes
Right Brete's chicken curry
Opposite Chicken, squash and sweet potato stew

BRETE'S CHICKEN CURRY

We added dried wide wheat noodles to our recipe for this curry that originated in the kitchens of the Muslim traders in Thailand.

3 tablespoons peanut oil
9 (2lb) boneless chicken thighs, sliced
1 large onion, sliced
1²/₃ cups coconut milk
8oz dried wheat noodles
5oz green beans, sliced

YELLOW CURRY PASTE
1 small red onion, chopped roughly
1¹/₂ tablespoons roughly chopped fresh lemon grass
4 cloves garlic, chopped coarsely
3 small fresh red chilis, seeded, chopped coarsely
1¹/₂ tablespoons roughly chopped fresh turmeric
1¹/₂ tablespoons roughly chopped fresh ginger
2 teaspoons coriander seeds
3 fresh cilantro roots, chopped coarsely

3 tablespoons fish sauce
3 kaffir lime leaves, torn
2 teaspoons sugar
3 tablespoons peanut oil

Heat oil in large pan; cook chicken, in batches, until browned. Cover to keep warm. Add onion to same pan; cook, stirring, until onion is soft. Add Yellow Curry Paste; cook, stirring, until fragrant. Return chicken to pan with coconut milk; simmer, uncovered, 30 minutes.

Meanwhile, cook noodles in large pan of boiling, salted water, uncovered, until just tender; drain.

Add beans to chicken curry in pan; cook, uncovered, until beans are just tender. Gently stir in noodles until just heated through.

Yellow Curry Paste Blend or process all ingredients until pureed.

SERVES 4

Brete's chicken curry is best made close to serving. Yellow curry paste can be made 1 week ahead

Storage In airtight container, in refrigerator
Freeze Yellow curry paste suitable

CHICKEN, SQUASH AND SWEET POTATO STEW

A fresh, quite wide egg noodle was our choice for this recipe, but any wheat noodle would suit, so long as it's fresh.

1lb fresh egg noodles
4 (1¹/₃lb) boneless chicken breasts
4 slices bacon, chopped
1¹/₂lb butternut squash, cut into 1-inch cubes
1¹/₂ tablespoons olive oil
1 small onion, chopped
1lb orange sweet potatoes, chopped
2 teaspoons chicken base or 2 bouillon cubes
2¹/₂ cups water
¹/₄ cup cream
1¹/₂ tablespoons fresh oregano

Place noodles in large heatproof bowl, cover with boiling water, let stand until just tender; drain.

Cook chicken on heated oiled griddle (or grill or barbecue) until chicken is browned both sides and tender. Remove chicken; slice into ¹/₂-inch pieces. Cover to keep warm.

Cook bacon on same griddle until crisp. Remove bacon; cover to keep warm.

Boil, steam or microwave squash pieces until just tender; drain. Cover to keep warm.

Meanwhile, heat oil in large pan; cook onion, stirring, until soft. Add sweet potato and blended bouillon powder or base and water to pan; cook, uncovered, until sweet potato is tender. Blend or process sweet potato mixture until smooth; stir in cream.

Gently toss noodles and chicken with squash, sweet potato mixture and two-thirds of the bacon in large bowl. Sprinkle with remaining bacon and oregano.

SERVES 6

Best made just before serving

CHICKEN FATTOUSH
WITH SOBA

Good food crosses all borders. Here the classic Syrian-Lebanese fattoush combines with wholesome Japanese soba to result in a dish that will be loved universally.

4 (1¹/₃lb) boneless chicken breasts
1 medium red onion
1 burpless cucumber
2-3 pocket pita breads (2oz each)
4oz soba (buckwheat noodles)
8oz cherry tomatoes, halved
1 large yellow bell pepper, seeded, sliced
¹/₂ cup roughly chopped fresh Italian parsley
¹/₄ cup roughly chopped fresh Italian parsley
3 tablespoons roughly chopped fresh mint
¹/₂ cup light olive oil
3 tablespoons lemon juice
2 teaspoons sumac [see Glossary] or tamarind concentrate
1¹/₂ teaspoons ground cumin
¹/₄ teaspoon ground cinnamon
1 clove garlic, crushed
¹/₂ teaspoon sugar

Cook chicken on heated oiled griddle (or grill or barbecue) until browned both sides and tender. Remove chicken; dice. Halve onion, cut into ¹/₂-inch wedges. Halve cucumber lengthwise; discard seeds, slice cucumber diagonally.

Toast pocket pita breads, uncovered, on oven rack at 400°F for about 15 minutes or until brown and crisp; break into pieces.

Cook noodles in large pan of boiling, salted water, uncovered, until just tender; drain. Rinse under cold water; drain.

Just before serving, gently toss chicken, onion, cucumber, pita pieces and noodles in large bowl with the tomatoes, bell pepper, herbs and combined remaining ingredients.

SERVES 6

Best made just before serving

CHICKEN, MUSHROOM AND VERMICELLI RISOTTO

The combination of risotto and mung bean thread noodles – commonly referred to as vermicelli – gives an interesting twist to this Italian classic.

5 cups chicken stock
1 cup dry white wine
1/4 cup olive oil
4 (1 1/3lb) boneless chicken breasts
2 tablespoons butter
4 cloves garlic, crushed
1 small leek, sliced
8oz button mushrooms, sliced
2oz fresh shiitake
mushrooms, sliced
2oz fresh oyster mushrooms, sliced
2 cups calrose rice
1/2 cup finely grated smoked
cheddar cheese
3 tablespoons chopped fresh chives
1 1/2 tablespoons chopped
fresh sage
vegetable oil, for deep-frying
4oz bean thread noodles

Add stock and wine to medium pan. Bring to boil; simmer, covered, until required.

Heat 1 1/2 tablespoons of the olive oil in large pan; cook chicken until browned both sides and tender. Remove chicken, cover; let stand 5 minutes. Dice chicken; cover to keep warm.

Heat remaining olive oil and butter in same pan; cook garlic, leek and mushrooms, stirring, until mushrooms are soft. Add rice; cook, stirring, 2 minutes or until translucent. Stir in 1/2 cup hot stock mixture; cook, stirring, about 3 minutes or until liquid is absorbed. Continue adding hot stock mixture, 1/2 cup at a time; cook, about 3 minutes or until liquid is absorbed, stirring between additions. Total cooking time will be about 35 minutes or until rice is just tender. Stir in chicken, cheese, chives and sage; cover the risotto to keep warm.

Heat vegetable oil in large pan; deep-fry noodles, in batches, until crisp. Drain noodles on paper towels.

Just before serving, stir noodles through risotto.

SERVES 4

Best made just before serving

▭ **SOBA** is made from buckwheat and varying proportions of wheat flour. A bowl of soba is the first meal of the year for many people in Japan, eaten at midnight to ensure good luck and health in the coming year. Hand-made soba is highly prized and soba masters are designated by the Japanese government with a hierarchy dictated by the number of years of experience.

Opposite Chicken fattoush with soba
Above Chicken, mushroom and vermicelli risotto

SESAME CHICKEN WITH MIXED GREEN VEGETABLES

We have used the crinkly noodle, originally from China, called ramen. Interestingly, they're the most popular noodle in Japan.

4 (1¹/₃lb) boneless chicken breasts, sliced
¹/₄ cup soy sauce
¹/₄ cup plum sauce
1¹/₂ tablespoons hoisin sauce
¹/₄ cup honey
¹/₄ cup dry sherry
8oz ramen noodles
8oz green beans, sliced
4oz snow peas
1¹/₂ tablespoons peanut oil
3 tablespoons cornstarch
4 green onions, chopped
5oz bean sprouts
1 teaspoon sesame oil
1 tablespoon sesame seeds, toasted

Place chicken in large bowl; pour combined sauces, honey and sherry over chicken, stir until coated in marinade. Cover; refrigerate 3 hours or overnight.

Cook noodles in large pan of boiling, salted water, uncovered, until just tender; drain. Rinse under cold water; drain.

Boil, steam or microwave beans and snow peas, separately, until just tender. Rinse under cold water; drain.

Drain chicken; reserve marinade. Heat peanut oil in wok or large pan; cook chicken, in batches, until browned both sides and tender. Add blended cornstarch and reserved marinade to pan; stir until mixture boils and thickens. Return chicken to pan with noodles, green beans, snow peas, onions, sprouts and sesame oil; stir-fry until just hot. Just before serving, sprinkle with sesame seeds.

SERVES 4 TO 6

Best made just before serving

RED PESTO CHICKEN WITH NOODLES

As you can see from our photograph, we used green-colored, spinach-flavored noodles; a plain wheat noodle or another flavor would work just as well.

10oz dried wheat noodles
1¹/₂ tablespoons olive oil
6 (2lb) boneless chicken breasts
1 medium onion, sliced
2 cloves garlic, crushed
¹/₄ cup dry red wine
3 tablespoons chopped fresh basil
1 cup chicken stock
²/₃ cup bottled pesto with basil and sun-dried sweet red bell peppers
¹/₃ cup coarsely grated parmesan cheese
4oz feta cheese, crumbled

Cook noodles in large pan of boiling, salted water, uncovered, until just tender; drain.

Heat oil in large pan; cook chicken, in batches, until browned both sides and tender. Cover; let stand 5 minutes. Cut into ¹/₃-inch slices; cover to keep warm.

Add onion and garlic to same pan; cook, stirring, until onion is soft. Stir in wine, basil, stock and pesto. Bring to boil; simmer about 5 minutes or until mixture thickens slightly. Add chicken and parmesan; stir until hot.

Just before serving, gently toss noodles with chicken mixture, sprinkle with feta.

SERVES 6

Best made just before serving

Opposite Sesame chicken with mixed green vegetables
Left Red pesto chicken with noodles

MEE KROB

This Thai crispy noodle dish with its sweet, sour and salty flavors has become a favorite in many of our homes. With the easy availability of these fine rice stick noodles, duplicating this restaurant treat in your own kitchen is a snap.

vegetable oil, for deep-frying
4oz dried rice noodles
2¹/2 tablespoons peanut oil
2 eggs, beaten
1¹/2 tablespoons water
1lb ground chicken
¹/4 cup lemon juice
3 tablespoons fish sauce
3 tablespoons tomato sauce
1 teaspoon soy sauce
3 tablespoons brown sugar
2 teaspoons chopped fresh
    red chilis
1 tablespoon chopped fresh cilantro
3 green onions, sliced
10oz firm tofu, cubed

Heat vegetable oil in large pan; deep-fry noodles, in batches, until puffed. Drain noodles on paper towels.

Heat 1 teaspoon of the peanut oil in wok or large pan; pour in half of the combined egg and water. Swirl heated pan to make a thin omelette; cook until just set. Transfer omelette to chopping board, roll tightly; cut into thin strips. Repeat with 1 more teaspoon of vegetable oil and remaining egg mixture.

Heat remaining oil in same pan; stir-fry chicken until browned and cooked through. Add combined juice, sauces, sugar, chili and cilantro; stir-fry 1 minute. Add onion, tofu and omelette strips; stir-fry until hot. Just before serving, gently toss noodles through chicken mixture.

SERVES 4 TO 6

Best made just before serving

Below Mee krob
Opposite Chicken and noodles in radicchio bowls

CHICKEN AND NOODLES IN RADICCHIO BOWLS

Try a variety of combinations: use a crisp, green lettuce rather than radicchio; or vegetable-flavored wide wheat noodles instead of plain ones.

3 tablespoons olive oil
3 (1lb) boneless chicken breasts
7oz dried wheat noodles
8oz tiny new potatoes, quartered
1 small sweet red bell pepper
1 small green bell pepper
4 slices bacon, chopped
4oz button mushrooms, sliced
8 large radicchio leaves

BUTTERMILK DRESSING
¹/2 cup olive oil
1¹/2 tablespoons Dijon mustard
3 tablespoons red wine vinegar
1 teaspoon sugar
1¹/2 tablespoons chopped
    fresh basil
2 cloves garlic, crushed
¹/2 cup buttermilk

Heat half the oil in large pan; cook chicken, in batches, until browned both sides and tender. Cover chicken; let stand 5 minutes. Cut into ¹/3-inch slices.

Cook noodles in large pan of boiling, salted water, uncovered, until just tender; drain. Cover to keep warm.

Boil, steam or microwave potatoes until just tender; drain. Halve bell peppers; remove and discard seeds and membranes, slice thinly.

Heat remaining oil in same pan; cook potatoes, stirring, until crisp and browned lightly. Remove from pan; cover to keep warm. Discard oil; add bacon to same pan; cook, stirring, until crisp. Drain on paper towels. Add peppers and mushrooms to same pan; cook, stirring, until just soft.

Gently toss chicken and noodles in large bowl with potatoes, bacon and pepper mixture. Just before serving, place 2 radicchio leaves on each of the 4 plates; divide chicken mixture among leaves, drizzle with Buttermilk Dressing.

Buttermilk Dressing Blend or process all ingredients until smooth.

SERVES 4

Best made just before serving

◻ **DRIED RICE NOODLES** Called beehoon in China and sen mee in Thailand (sen means line, mee means thin), these fine noodles are the mainstay of a Malaysian laksa. Usually soaked in hot water for 5 minutes before use, except when making crispy noodle dishes such as mee krob where the step is unnecessary.

CRUNCHY NOODLE PIZZAS

Everyone knows Marco Polo took noodles from China to Italy but few would have guessed that they'd end up on a pizza.

1¹/₂ tablespoons vegetable oil
8 (1³/₄lb) boneless chicken thighs
2 10-inch packaged pizza crusts
7oz fried noodles, crushed lightly
**2 cups coarsely grated
    mozzarella cheese**
¹/₂ cup sweet chili sauce
3 tablespoons soy sauce

PESTO

2 cups firmly packed fresh basil
**¹/₄ cup blanched almonds,
    toasted, chopped**
2 cloves garlic, crushed
¹/₃ cup olive oil

Heat oil in large pan; cook chicken, in batches, until browned both sides and tender. Drain chicken on paper towels; cut into ¹/₄-inch slices.

Spread Pesto evenly over pizza crusts; top with chicken. Sprinkle combined noodles and cheese over chicken; drizzle with combined sauces. Bake at 350°F for about 20 minutes or until pizza tops are browned and edges are crisp.

Pesto Blend or process all ingredients until smooth.

SERVES 6 TO 8

Best made just before serving

CHICKEN SPINACH LASAGNA

Fresh rice noodle sheets, measure about 16 x 28 inches when unfolded; there are usually 2 sheets to a 2lb package. They don't need pre-cooking for this recipe.

3 tablespoons olive oil
6 (2lb) boneless chicken breasts
2 medium onions, sliced
2 cloves garlic, crushed
8oz button mushrooms, sliced
1lb spinach
7 tablespoons butter
¹/₂ cup all-purpose flour
2¹/₂ cups milk
¹/₄ cup dry white wine
1 egg yolk
**¹/₂ cup coarsely grated
    romano cheese**
1lb fresh rice noodle sheet

Heat half the oil in large pan; cook chicken, in batches, until browned both sides and tender. Cover; let stand 5 minutes. Cut into ¹/₃-inch slices.

Add onions and garlic to same pan; cook, stirring, until onions are soft. Remove from pan.

Heat remaining oil in same pan; cook mushrooms, stirring, until just soft. Drain on paper towels.

Boil, steam or microwave spinach until wilted; rinse under cold water. Press out excess liquid; drain on paper towels.

Melt butter in medium pan; stir in flour until bubbling. Remove from the heat; gradually stir in milk, then wine. Stir over heat until white sauce boils and thickens. Remove from heat; stir egg yolk and half the cheese into white sauce.

Cut noodle sheets into 9 pieces, each measuring 5 x 7 inches. Place 3 noodle pieces over base of oiled 10-cup (2¹/₂ quart) ovenproof dish. Spread half the chicken, spinach, onion mixture and mushrooms over noodles; cover with 3 noodle pieces and half the white sauce. Repeat layering with remaining chicken, spinach, onion mixture and mushrooms, finishing with the last 3 noodle pieces. Pour remaining white sauce over noodles, sprinkle with remaining cheese.

Bake, uncovered, at 350°F for about 45 minutes, or until top is browned.

SERVES 6

Can be made 1 day ahead

Storage Covered, in refrigerator

SPANISH CHILI CHICKEN

Arroz con pollo, rice with chicken, is one of Spain's most famous dishes. Here, we swap the rice for dried wide egg noodles and find it's just as aromatically delicious.

1¹/₂ tablespoons olive oil
9 (3lb) boneless chicken thighs
2 (12oz) chorizo sausages, sliced
1 large red onion, sliced
4 cloves garlic, crushed
2 teaspoons ground cumin
2 teaspoons sweet paprika
4 large (2lb) tomatoes,
    peeled, chopped
1 cup chicken stock
3 tablespoons hot chili sauce
3 tablespoons chopped
    fresh oregano
3 tablespoons lemon juice
8oz dried egg noodles

Heat oil in large pan; cook chicken, in batches, until browned both sides and tender. Discard fat from chicken. Add chorizo to same pan; cook until browned. Add onion and garlic; cook, stirring, until onion is soft. Add cumin and paprika; cook, stirring, until fragrant. Stir in tomatoes, stock, sauce, oregano and juice. Return chicken to pan. Bring to boil; simmer, covered, about 30 minutes or until chicken is tender.

Meanwhile, cook noodles in large pan of boiling, salted water, uncovered, until just tender; drain. Just before serving, gently toss noodles with chicken mixture.

SERVES 6 TO 8

Best made just before serving

◖ **BIRTHDAY NOODLES** In China, noodles are a symbol of longevity and are often served at birthday parties and as a "crossing the threshold to a new year" food. They are, of course, also eaten at weddings, funerals and just about any other occasion when hunger dictates the serving of food.

Opposite Crunchy noodle pizzas
Left Chicken spinach lasagna
Below Spanish chili chicken

LARB-STYLE CHICKEN

Larb is a well-known Thai dish and its complex flavors combine to make a unique main course. We used boneless chicken breasts rather than ground chicken in our version.

4 (1¹/₃lb) boneless chicken breasts
1 burpless cucumber
8oz asparagus, trimmed
5oz dried rice noodles
3 green onions, sliced
1 medium sweet red bell pepper, seeded, sliced
3oz bean sprouts
¹/₃ cup unsalted peanuts, toasted, chopped
¹/₄ cup chopped fresh mint
3 tablespoons chopped fresh cilantro
¹/₃ cup lime juice
¹/₄ cup vegetable oil
3 tablespoons finely chopped fresh lemon grass
3 small fresh red chilis, seeded, finely sliced
2 tablespoons fish sauce
2 teaspoons brown sugar
1 clove garlic, crushed

Cook chicken on heated oiled griddle (or grill or barbecue) until browned both sides and tender. Remove from pan; cut into ¹/₃-inch slices. Halve the cucumber lengthwise; discard seeds, cut into ¹/₃-inch slices. Cut asparagus into 1¹/₂-inch lengths; boil, steam or microwave until just tender. Rinse asparagus under cold water; drain.

Place noodles in large heatproof bowl, cover with boiling water, let stand until just tender. Rinse under cold water; drain.

Combine chicken and noodles in large bowl with cucumber, asparagus, onion, pepper, sprouts, half the peanuts and herbs. Just before serving, gently toss in combined remaining ingredients.

SERVES 6

Best made just before serving

Right Larb-style chicken
Opposite Char kway teow

CHAR KWAY TEOW

The classic Malaysian fried noodle dish travels easily to our kitchens now that fresh rice noodles are so easy to obtain. Make sure you purchase fresh noodles; otherwise they may break when you try to cut them.

2lb fresh rice noodle sheets
1lb small uncooked prawns
$1/4$ cup peanut oil
2 (12oz) boneless chicken breasts, chopped
4 small fresh red chilis, seeded, chopped
2 cloves garlic, crushed
2 teaspoons grated fresh ginger
2 eggs, beaten
5 green onions, sliced
5oz bean sprouts
$1 1/2$ tablespoons light soy sauce
1 teaspoon thick teriyaki sauce
$1/4$ cup dark soy sauce
$1/4$ teaspoon sesame oil
1 teaspoon brown sugar

Cut noodle sheets into $3/4$-inch strips. Place noodles in large bowl, cover with warm water; gently separate with hands. Let noodles stand for 1 minute; drain.

Shell and devein prawns, leaving tails intact; halve prawns crosswise.

Heat $1 1/2$ tablespoons of the peanut oil in wok or large pan; stir-fry chicken, chili, garlic and ginger about 2 minutes or until chicken is tender. Remove from pan; cover.

Heat half the remaining peanut oil in same pan; stir-fry prawns about 2 minutes or until prawns change color. Remove from pan; cover. Add eggs, onion and sprouts to same pan; stir-fry until egg is just set. Remove from pan; cover.

Add remaining peanut oil to same pan; stir-fry noodles and combined remaining ingredients 1 minute. Return chicken, prawns and egg mixture to pan; stir-fry until hot.

SERVES 6

Best made just before serving

Fishing for compliments

 If the noodle is a canvas, seafood is the ingredient that can elevate a simple dish to a work of art. We have many choices of both fish and shellfish. This haul of recipes pays tribute to that bounty as it spans the menu from starters to main courses.

LIME AND WASABI SEAFOOD NOODLES

Use baby beet leaves for their color, if available; however, baby spinach leaves can be substituted with no loss of flavor. We used a yellow, vegetable-dyed, dried wheat noodle for its color; experiment with different-colored wheat noodles just for the effect.

1¹/2lb **medium uncooked prawns**
1¹/2lb **baby octopus**
8oz **dried wheat noodles**
8oz **scallops**
4oz **baby beet leaves**
¹/2 **cup peanut oil**
1¹/2 **tablespoons cider vinegar**
2¹/2 **teaspoons wasabi**
2 **teaspoons finely grated lime rind**
1 **clove garlic, crushed**

Shell and devein prawns, leaving tails intact. Discard heads and beaks from octopus; cut octopus in half.

Cook noodles in large pan of boiling salted water, uncovered, until just tender; drain. Cover to keep warm.

Cook seafood, in batches, on heated oiled griddle (or grill or barbecue) until just cooked.

Combine seafood and noodles in large bowl with beet leaves and combined remaining ingredients.

SERVES 4 TO 6

Best made just before serving

SOBA WITH PRAWN TEMPURA

Traditional tempura takes a Western turn with this chilled vegetable and soba dish. Beautiful buckwheat soba is just one of several Japanese noodles we have adopted; watch out for them in all Asian food shops.

8oz soba
1 medium carrot
4 green onions
1 medium sweet red bell pepper
1 medium yellow bell pepper
1 medium green bell pepper
1¹/₂ tablespoons sesame seeds, toasted
2lb medium uncooked prawns
1 egg yolk
1¹/₄ cups iced water
1 cup all-purpose flour
extra all-purpose flour
vegetable oil, for deep-frying
2 sheets nori, cut into ¹/₄-inch pieces

LEMON SOY DRESSING
¹/₂ cup peanut oil
1¹/₂ tablespoons soy sauce
1¹/₂ tablespoons seasoned rice vinegar
1 teaspoon wasabi
¹/₂ teaspoon sesame oil
3 tablespoons lemon juice

Cook noodles in large pan of boiling salted water, uncovered, until just tender; drain. Rinse under cold water; drain.

Cut carrot and onions into very thin, 3-inch-long strips. Halve bell peppers; remove and discard seeds and membranes. Slice peppers into very thin strips.

Gently toss noodles, carrot, onion and peppers in large bowl with sesame seeds and Lemon Soy Dressing; refrigerate while making prawn tempura.

Shell and devein prawns, leaving tails intact. Cut prawns along back almost all the way through; flatten slightly.

Just before serving, combine egg yolk and water in medium bowl; stir in sifted flour all at once. Do not overmix; mixture should be lumpy. Roll prawns in extra flour, shake off excess.

Heat vegetable oil in large pan. Dip prawns, in batches, in batter; deep-fry until prawns are cooked and browned lightly. Drain on paper towels. Deep-fry nori in same hot oil until just crisp; drain on paper towels.

Divide cold soba mixture among serving plates; top with prawn tempura, sprinkle with nori.

Lemon Soy Dressing Place ingredients in medium bowl; whisk until well combined.

SERVES 6

Prawn tempura must be made just before serving. Soba can be prepared 3 hours ahead

Storage Covered, in refrigerator

Above Soba with prawn tempura
Opposite Baked trout with orange hazelnut glaze

BAKED TROUT WITH ORANGE HAZELNUT GLAZE

The subtle nature of this fish calls for an equally delicate noodle, so we used a vermicelli-like, extra-thin wheat noodle.

10oz dried wheat noodles
2 tablespoons butter
1 large carrot, sliced finely
1 medium leek, sliced finely
1 teaspoon finely grated
**   orange rind**
2/3 cup hazelnuts, toasted, chopped
4 whole rainbow trout
2 tablespoons butter, extra
1 cup orange juice

Cook noodles in large pan of boiling salted water, uncovered, until just tender; drain. Rinse under cold water; drain.

Melt butter in medium pan; cook carrot and leek, stirring, until soft. Stir in noodles, rind and half the nuts; divide noodle mixture in half.

Divide one of the halves of the noodle mixture equally among the cavities of each trout; place filled trout, in single layer, in greased baking dish. Bake, uncovered, at 350°F about 20 minutes or until cooked through.

Meanwhile, melt extra butter in small pan, add juice; simmer, uncovered, about 5 minutes or until mixture is reduced by a third. Stir remaining nuts into glaze.

Reheat remaining noodle mixture in medium pan. Serve trout over noodle mixture with glaze.

SERVES 4

Best made just before serving

SOBA comes in varying proportions of buckwheat and wheat flour, usually between 20% to 40% buckwheat. The color varies accordingly, from brownish through to almost white, with cha-soba, to which powdered tea is added, being quite green. There are many claims for soba's health benefits, so it is often served as a kind of digestive at the end of a multi-course meal.

MIXED SEAFOOD
IN A PUMPKIN BASKET

*We used a straight ramen variety here, but
any dried wheat noodle can be pre-cooked
just before being mixed into the filling.*

4 large (3³/₄lb) sugar pumpkins
6 small black mussels
16 (1lb) medium
uncooked prawns
4 (8oz) small squid,
tentacles removed
1 teaspoon vegetable oil
4 cloves garlic, crushed
2 teaspoons grated fresh galangal
1¹/₂ tablespoons chopped fresh
lemon grass
1²/₃ cups coconut milk
1¹/₂ tablespoons fish sauce
3 tablespoons mild chili sauce
1/₃ cup firmly packed fresh cilantro
2 kaffir lime leaves, torn
20 (1lb) large white scallops
5oz ramen

Place whole pumpkins on oiled oven tray;
bake, uncovered, in 400°F oven about
45 minutes, or until tender.

Meanwhile, scrub mussels and remove
beards. Shell and devein prawns, leaving
tails intact. Cut squid in half; lightly score
inside surface with a criss-cross pattern,
cut into 1-inch pieces.

Save tops and seeds of pumpkins for
other uses. Scoop out pumpkin to within
1/₄ inch of skin; reserve 1 cup pumpkin,
save remainder for another use. Cover
pumpkin to keep warm.

Heat oil in medium pan; cook garlic,
galangal and lemon grass, stirring, about
1 minute. Add milk, sauces, cilantro and
reserved pumpkin. Blend or process
coconut mixture until almost smooth.
Return coconut mixture to same pan;
bring to boil. Add lime leaves and all
seafood; simmer, stirring occasionally,
until seafood is just tender and changed
in color.

Just before serving, cook noodles in
large pan of boiling salted water,
uncovered, until just tender; drain.
Gently toss noodles into seafood mixture
in pan; divide mixture among pumpkins.
SERVES 4

Best made just before serving

CREAMY LIME NOODLES
WITH SMOKED SALMON

*A refined wheat noodle such as somen
is a perfect choice for this light yet flavorful
dish. Odd pieces, or ends, of smoked
salmon are both economical and
well-suited to this recipe.*

1lb dried wheat noodles
1¹/₂ tablespoons peanut oil
1/₂ small red onion, chopped finely
2 small fresh red chilis,
seeded, chopped
1¹/₂ tablespoons finely grated
lime rind
1¹/₂ tablespoons lime juice
2¹/₃ cups light cream
1/₂ cup chopped macadamias,
toasted
8oz smoked salmon, chopped
4oz arugula, trimmed

Cook noodles in large pan of boiling
salted water, uncovered, until just
tender; drain. Cover to keep warm.

Heat oil in wok or large pan; stir-fry
onion, chili and rind until onion is soft.
Stir in juice, cream, nuts and salmon;
simmer until sauce thickens slightly.

Just before serving, gently toss
noodles and arugula in large bowl with
salmon cream mixture.

SERVES 4 TO 6

Best made just before serving

CRAB, GOAT CHEESE AND CHIVE ROSTI

These exquisite patties, accompanied by a green salad, make a perfect light lunch. The thin fresh egg noodles we used complement the clean, mild flavor of the dish.

5oz fresh egg noodles
6 eggs, beaten
1/2 cup cream
1/4 cup all-purpose flour
1lb fresh crab meat, shredded
8oz firm mild goat cheese, crumbled
1/4 cup chopped fresh chives

Cook noodles in large pan of boiling salted water, uncovered, until just tender; drain. Rinse under cold water; drain. Chop noodles coarsely.

Combine eggs and cream in large bowl; gradually stir in flour. Stir in noodles, crab, cheese and chives.

Coat 3-inch egg rings with cooking oil spray; place in large heated oiled pan. Place 1/4 cup of rosti mixture into each ring; cook, on both sides, until browned and cooked through.

Repeat with remaining rosti mixture.

MAKES ABOUT 24

Best made just before serving

Opposite Mixed seafood in a pumpkin basket
Above Creamy lime noodles with smoked salmon
Right Crab, goat cheese and chive rosti

PHAD THAI

We used sen lek, the 1/4-inch-wide rice stick noodle traditionally used in this Thai classic. You can substitute poultry, if you prefer, for the prawns and pork, or make a vegetarian pad Thai using deep-fried tofu.

12oz dried rice noodles
1/4 cup brown sugar
2 teaspoons soy sauce
1 1/2 tablespoons tomato sauce
1/4 cup mild chili sauce
1/4 cup fish sauce
1 1/2 tablespoons peanut oil
8oz ground pork
2 cloves garlic, crushed
1 1/2 tablespoons grated
    fresh ginger
3 eggs, beaten
8oz medium cooked
    prawns, shelled
2 teaspoons chopped fresh
    red chilis
2 green onions, sliced

BARBECUED OCTOPUS WITH STRINGHOPPERS

The Sri Lankan stringhopper is an indigenous "noodle" to the subcontinent where, not unlike pappadums, it is more often purchased from specialist makers than prepared from scratch at home. Look for them in Indian and Sri Lankan food shops.

2lb baby octopus
1/4 cup lemon juice
1 clove garlic, crushed
2 corn cobs
8oz cherry tomatoes, halved
8oz curly endive, chopped
3 tablespoons lemon juice, extra
1/4 cup light olive oil
1 1/2 tablespoons sweet chili sauce
1 1/2 tablespoons chopped
    fresh mint
vegetable oil, for deep-frying
5oz stringhoppers

Remove and discard heads and beaks from octopus; cut in half. Combine octopus with lemon juice and garlic in large bowl. Cover; refrigerate 30 minutes.

Remove husks from corn. Boil, steam or microwave corn until just tender; drain. Chop corn into 1 1/2-inch pieces; cut pieces into quarters.

Drain octopus; discard marinade. Cook octopus, in batches, on heated oiled griddle (or grill or barbecue) until just cooked. Cook tomatoes on same griddle until just softened.

Gently toss octopus, corn and tomatoes in large bowl with endive and combined extra juice, olive oil, sauce and mint in large bowl.

Heat vegetable oil in large pan; deep-fry stringhoppers until puffed. Drain on paper towels. Serve octopus mixture with stringhoppers.

SERVES 4 TO 6

Stringhoppers must be deep-fried just before serving. Octopus can be marinated 1 day ahead

Storage Covered, in refrigerator

5oz bean sprouts
2 tablespoons chopped
   fresh cilantro
1/2 cup unsalted roasted peanuts,
   chopped

Place noodles in large heatproof bowl,
cover with boiling salted water, let stand
until just tender; drain. Cover noodles to
keep warm.

Combine sugar and sauces in small
pan; cook, stirring, until sugar dissolves.

Heat oil in wok or large pan; stir-fry
pork, garlic and ginger until pork is
browned and almost cooked. Add eggs
and prawns; cook, stirring gently, until
egg sets. Add noodles, sauce mixture and
remaining ingredients; gently stir-fry
until hot. If desired, serve Phad Thai with
fresh lime wedges.

SERVES 4 TO 6

Best made just before serving

Left Barbecued octopus with stringhoppers
Below Phad Thai
Right South Indian grilled fish with
coconut masala

SOUTH INDIAN GRILLED FISH WITH COCONUT MASALA

*While we used barramundi here, you can
substitute perch or snapper fish, cut into
steaks or fillets, for this recipe. The fresh
wheat noodle pictured is lei mein, which
differs only from chow mein in that it is
slightly heavier and more dense.*

1/4 cup firmly packed fresh
   Italian parsley
1/4 cup firmly packed fresh cilantro
3 tablespoons lemon juice
3 tablespoons olive oil
1 1/2 tablespoons ground cumin
1 teaspoon ground coriander
1/2 teaspoon sweet paprika
1/4 teaspoon ground cinnamon
2 cloves garlic, chopped
1 small fresh red chili,
   seeded, chopped
1/2 teaspoon salt
3/4 cup coconut milk powder
1 1/4 cups warm water
4 6oz fish steaks
1 1/2lb fresh wheat noodles

Blend or process fresh herbs, lemon juice,
oil, ground spices, garlic, chili and salt
until smooth. Place herb mixture in
medium pan with blended milk powder
and water. Bring to boil; simmer, stirring,
1 minute.

Cook fish on heated oiled griddle (or
grill or barbecue) until browned both
sides and cooked through.

Meanwhile, cook noodles in large pan
of boiling salted water, uncovered, until
just tender; drain.

Divide noodles among each of the
serving plates; top with fish, then heated
coconut masala.

SERVES 4

Best made just before serving

◧ **STRINGHOPPERS** are a Sri Lankan
specialty, made by forcing a rice-flour
batter through a perforated mould to
form a lacy circle about the size of a
saucer. Eaten as an accompaniment to a
rich main course, stringhoppers are tricky
to make but, fortunately, instant dried
versions are available at Asian food shops.

SZECHUAN PRAWNS WITH NOODLE POLENTA BATONS

Fettuccine-like fresh egg noodles are chopped and mixed with polenta and pecorino to make crunchy batons that are a perfect foil for these spicy prawns. Coarsely grated parmesan or dry jack cheeses may be substituted if pecorino cheese is unavailable.

20 (2lb) large uncooked prawns
3 tablespoons dry sherry
2 teaspoons sugar
1¹/₂ tablespoons cider vinegar
8oz fresh egg noodles
1 cup vegetable stock
¹/₂ cup water
¹/₂ cup polenta
¹/₂ teaspoon salt
¹/₄ cup grated pecorino cheese
1¹/₂ tablespoons sesame oil
4 medium plum tomatoes, sliced
2oz arugula, trimmed
3 tablespoons sweet chili sauce
1¹/₂ tablespoons dark soy sauce
1¹/₂ tablespoons lime juice

Shell and devein prawns, leaving tails intact. Combine sherry, sugar, vinegar and prawns in medium bowl. Cover; refrigerate 1 hour.

Place noodles in medium heatproof bowl, cover with boiling water, let noodles stand until just tender; drain. Chop noodles coarsely.

Bring stock and water to boil in medium pan. Gradually stir in polenta and salt; cook, stirring, over low heat about 2 minutes or until mixture is thickened slightly. Stir in noodles and cheese. Pour into oiled deep 8-inch square cake pan. Cover; refrigerate until firm.

Just before serving, turn polenta onto board. Cut polenta in half; cut each half, crosswise, into 1-inch strips. Brush polenta batons with sesame oil; cook, in batches, on heated oiled griddle until golden brown both sides. Cover to keep warm. Cook prawns on same griddle until they change color. Serve prawns with polenta batons, tomato and arugula; drizzle over combined remaining ingredients.

SERVES 4

Polenta mixture can be prepared 1 day ahead

Storage Covered, in refrigerator

Opposite Szechuan prawns with noodle polenta batons
Right Siberian salmon with soba blini

SIBERIAN SALMON WITH SOBA BLINI

It's perfectly natural to make blini with soba since these tiny Russian pancakes are traditionally made of buckwheat flour – the main ingredient in soba.

4oz soba
6 eggs, beaten
2/3 cup water
3 tablespoons fish sauce
1¹/2 tablespoons wasabi
1 sheet toasted nori, shredded
1¹/4 cups sour cream
1¹/2 tablespoons chopped fresh dill
1 small red onion, chopped
1¹/2 tablespoons olive oil
4 7oz Atlantic salmon fillets
3 tablespoons lemon juice
3 tablespoons vodka
4 tablespoons butter

Cook noodles in large pan of boiling salted water, uncovered, until just tender; drain. Rinse under cold water; drain. Cut into 1-inch lengths.

Whisk eggs with water in large bowl until frothy; stir in fish sauce and wasabi.

Gently toss noodles and nori into egg mixture. Heat oiled 8-inch crepe pan; add about ¹/3 cup of egg mixture to pan, swirl to coat base. Cook until blini is set underneath then grill until top is just set; carefully slide blini onto board. Repeat with remaining egg mixture; you need 8 blini for this recipe.

Stack two blini; roll tightly in plastic wrap, secure ends. Repeat with remaining blini. Mix cream, dill and onion in small bowl; cover, refrigerate until required.

Just before serving, heat olive oil in large pan; cook salmon, in batches, until browned both sides and cooked as desired. Cover to keep warm. Add juice, vodka and butter to same pan; stir until butter melts.

Unwrap the blini parcels; cut each into 3 pieces. Divide blini pieces among serving plates with salmon, sour cream mixture and vodka butter sauce.

SERVES 4

Blini and sour cream mixture can be made 3 hours ahead

Storage Covered, separately, in refrigerator

POLENTA-PEPPERED TUNA WITH RICE NOODLE RIBBONS

For this recipe, we used 1 of the 2 fresh rice noodle sheets that are sold already packaged in 2lb bags, folded into pleats and sliced into 1/2-inch ribbons.

4 1-inch-thick tuna steaks
1/4 cup polenta
2 tablespoons coarsely ground black pepper
vegetable oil, for shallow-frying
1lb fresh rice noodles, 1/2-inch wide

BASIL DRESSING
1/3 cup light olive oil
1/3 cup olive oil
1/4 cup firmly packed fresh basil
3 tablespoons lemon juice
1 1/2 tablespoons Dijon mustard
2 teaspoons honey

Brush tuna with water; coat in combined polenta and pepper. Heat oil in large pan; fry tuna, in batches, until browned both sides and cooked through.

Place noodles in large pan of boiling salted water, remove immediately; drain. Gently toss noodles in large bowl with a third of the Basil Dressing; divide noodles among serving plates. Top with tuna; drizzle with remaining dressing.

Basil Dressing Blend or process all ingredients until smooth.

SERVES 4

Best made just before serving

Below Polenta-peppered tuna with rice noodle ribbons
Right Coco-chili prawns on a noodle nest

◪ **FRESH RICE NOODLE SHEETS** are a thoroughly versatile product, being used whole for lasagne-type dishes, cut into small rounds or squares for tortellini or ravioli, torn into fragments for "rag" pasta, or cut into long strips. To make noodles, gently unwrap the sheet, smoothing out any wrinkles. Fold sheet into thirds, then in half. Trim edges, then cut into the desired width.

COCO-CHILLI PRAWNS ON A NOODLE NEST

We used bundles of thin dried wheat noodles here, but any dried noodle – even bean thread – can be deep-fried for the desired effect of the prawns' nests.

30 (1¹/₂lb) medium
   uncooked prawns
1¹/₂ tablespoons peanut oil
1 large onion, sliced
2 cloves garlic, crushed
2 teaspoons grated fresh ginger
1¹/₂ tablespoons black
   mustard seeds
1¹/₂ tablespoons ground cumin

1¹/₂ tablespoons ground coriander
2 small fresh red chilis, seeded,
   chopped finely
4 fresh curry leaves, torn
1²/₃ cups coconut milk
¹/₂ cup water
1 tablespoon chopped fresh cilantro
vegetable oil, for deep-frying
6 bunches (8oz) dried
   wheat noodles

Shell and devein prawns, leaving tails intact. Heat peanut oil in large pan; cook onion, garlic and ginger, stirring, until onion is soft. Add seeds, cumin, coriander, chili and curry leaves; cook, stirring, until seeds pop. Add combined milk and water. Bring to boil; simmer, uncovered, about 5 minutes or until sauce thickens. Add prawns; simmer, uncovered, about 5 minutes or until prawns change color and are just cooked. Stir in cilantro.

Heat vegetable oil in large pan; deep-fry noodle bunches until puffed and browned lightly. Drain noodle bunches on paper towels. Serve prawn mixture on noodle nests.

SERVES 4 TO 6

Best made just before serving

CAJUN-STYLE FISH WRAPPED IN BANANA LEAVES

We used cod here because it stands up to the cajun spices but you can use any firm white fish fillet when making this recipe.

4 large banana leaves
13oz orange sweet potato, sliced thinly
1 teaspoon salt
1 teaspoon hot paprika
1 teaspoon cracked black pepper
1 teaspoon ground cumin
1 teaspoon ground oregano
4 (2lb) boneless white fish fillets
12oz fresh rice noodles
1 teaspoon peanut oil
2 teaspoons chopped fresh lemon grass
1 small fresh red chili, seeded, chopped finely
1 cup coconut milk
1 tablespoon chopped fresh cilantro
2 teaspoons lime juice

Cut each banana leaf into a 14-inch square. Using tongs, submerge the squares, 1 leaf at a time, in large pan of boiling water; remove immediately. Rinse leaves under cold water; dry thoroughly. Leaves should be soft and pliable.

Boil, steam or microwave sweet potato until almost tender; drain.

Combine salt, paprika, pepper, cumin and oregano in medium bowl; coat fish fillets in spice mixture.

Place noodles in large heatproof bowl, cover with boiling salted water, let stand until just tender; drain.

Divide noodles and sweet potato among banana leaves; top with fish fillets. Fold opposite sides of leaves over fish fillets; repeat with remaining sides.

Place parcels, seam-side down, in single layer, in greased baking dish. Bake, uncovered, at 350°F about 35 minutes or until fish is tender.

Meanwhile, heat oil in small pan; cook lemon grass and chili, stirring, 1 minute. Stir in milk, cilantro and juice. Bring to boil; simmer, uncovered, about 2 minutes or until sauce thickens slightly.

Place fish parcels, seam-side up, on serving plates; open out corners of banana leaves slightly, drizzle fish with warm coconut sauce.

SERVES 4

Best made just before serving

NOODLE AND PRAWN CHERMOULLA

Chermoulla is just one of the many Moroccan flavors that has crept into our kitchen today. Used as a marinade or sauce, like salsa or masala, it is made of herbs and spices according to the taste of the individual cook but almost always contains fresh cilantro, cumin and paprika.

40 (2lb) medium uncooked prawns
5oz dried rice noodles
3 tablespoons olive oil
5 medium (2lb) tomatoes, peeled, seeded, sliced
1/4 cup roughly chopped fresh Italian parsley

CHERMOULLA
1/3 cup firmly packed fresh cilantro
1/3 cup firmly packed fresh Italian parsley
1/4 cup olive oil
3 tablespoons lemon juice
2 small fresh red chilis, seeded, chopped
2 cloves garlic, chopped
2 teaspoons ground cumin
1 teaspoon sweet paprika
1 teaspoon ground coriander
1/2 teaspoon salt

Shell and devein prawns, leaving tails intact. Combine prawns with half the Chermoulla in medium bowl. Cover; refrigerate 3 hours or overnight.

Place noodles in medium heatproof bowl, cover with boiling salted water, stand only until just tender; drain.

Just before serving, heat oil in wok or large pan; stir-fry prawns until changed in color and almost cooked. Add noodles; stir-fry until hot. Remove from heat. Gently toss prawn mixture in large bowl with remaining Chermoulla, tomato and parsley.

Chermoulla Blend or process all ingredients until almost pureed.

SERVES 4

Prawns best marinated 1 day ahead

Storage Covered, in refrigerator

⊏ **IDENTITY CRISES** Many words — soba, udon, ramen, mee, kway teow, mein, bee hoon and sen, to name a few — either actually mean, or incorporate the sense of, "noodle" in their translations. Therefore, in recipes and on menus, it would be repetitive to follow the name with the word noodle. So when you see a dish called yum wun sen, zaru-soba, mee krob or char kway teow, you automatically know it's a noodle dish.

ORIENTAL CHILI SQUID PACKAGES

We used mung bean thread noodles to help bind the squid filling, but a thin fresh rice noodle would work just as well.

14 dried shiitake mushrooms
8oz bean thread noodles
1¹/₂ tablespoons vegetable oil
4 cloves garlic, crushed
1¹/₂ tablespoons chopped fresh
    lemon grass
8oz can water chestnuts,
    drained, chopped
8 green onions, chopped
3 tablespoons chopped fresh mint
8oz shelled cooked prawns, chopped
¹/₄ cup sweet chili sauce
¹/₄ cup teriyaki sauce
10 medium (1³/₄lb) squid,
    tentacles removed
3 teaspoons salt
3 tablespoons sugar
¹/₃ cup mild chili powder
3 tablespoons ground ginger
3 tablespoons vegetable oil, extra
¹/₃ cup chopped fresh cilantro
⁵/₈ cup butter, melted

Place mushrooms in small heatproof bowl, cover with boiling water, let stand about 20 minutes or until soft; drain. Discard stems; chop caps finely.

Place noodles in medium heatproof bowl, cover with boiling water, let stand until just tender; drain. Cut noodles into 1¹/₂-inch lengths.

Heat oil in large pan; cook garlic, lemon grass and water chestnuts, stirring, until fragrant. Add mushrooms, noodles, onion, mint, prawns and sauces; stir until combined. Fill squid with noodle mixture; secure openings with skewers. Combine salt, sugar, chili powder and ginger in large plastic bag; shake filled squid in bag, 1 at a time, to coat in spice mixture.

Place squid in large greased baking dish, in single layer; drizzle with extra oil. Bake, uncovered, at 350°F about 40 minutes or until squid is tender. Serve with combined cilantro and butter.

SERVES 4 TO 6

Filled squid best cooked just before serving but can be prepared up to 3 hours ahead

Storage Covered, in refrigerator

Opposite Cajun-style fish wrapped in banana leaves
Above Noodle and prawn chermoulla
Left Oriental chili squid packages

FRESH SALMON, CAPER AND DILL FRITTATA

The wholesomeness of creamy-white udon is the perfect match for that delectable combination of salmon, dill, capers and cream. A thin fresh egg noodle can be substituted if you cannot find Japanese udon in your area. Start with salmon either in a single piece or as fillets because it's ultimately to be flaked in the frittata.

1¹/₂ tablespoons olive oil
1lb Atlantic salmon
1 medium onion, sliced
5oz dried udon

6 eggs, beaten
³/₄ cup cream
1¹/₂ tablespoons chopped fresh dill
¹/₄ cup capers, chopped
¹/₄ teaspoon cracked black pepper
³/₄ cup light sour cream
1¹/₂ tablespoons drained green peppercorns, chopped

Oil a deep 11-inch-round cake pan, line base with parchment.

Heat oil in large pan; cook salmon until browned both sides and just cooked through. Remove from pan; break with fork into large flakes. Add onion to same pan; cook until soft.

Cook noodles in large pan of boiling salted water, uncovered, until just tender; drain. Rinse under cold water; drain.

Combine eggs with cream in large bowl; gently stir in salmon, onion, noodles, dill, capers and black pepper. Pour frittata mixture into prepared pan; bake, uncovered, at 350°F about 30 minutes or until set. Let frittata stand 5 minutes before turning out; serve with combined sour cream and peppercorns.

SERVES 4

Best made just before serving

SHANGHAIED PRAWNS AND STIR-FRIED VEGETABLES

We wrapped these prawns in fresh Shanghai noodles, made of wheat flour, which need no pre-cooking before being deep-fried around the seafood.

**30 (1½lb) medium
    uncooked prawns
1 clove garlic, crushed
3 tablespoons lemon juice
3 tablespoons sweet chili sauce
2 teaspoons soy sauce
1½ tablespoons chopped
    fresh cilantro
8oz fresh Shanghai noodles
3 medium carrots
3 medium sweet red bell
    peppers, seeded
3 green onions, trimmed
vegetable oil, for deep-frying
1½ tablespoons butter
1½ tablespoons peanut oil
3 cloves garlic, crushed, extra
8oz bean sprouts
1 teaspoon soy sauce, extra**

Shell and devein prawns, leaving tails intact. Combine prawns with garlic, juice, sauces and cilantro in medium bowl. Cover; refrigerate 3 hours or overnight.

Drain prawns; discard marinade.

Place noodles flat on tray to make them easier to handle. Pick up 2 noodles, loop them around prawn tail to secure; wrap noodles around prawn to cover. If first 2 noodles are not long enough to cover whole prawn, pick up 2 more, pressing their ends at loose ends of original 2 noodles to secure. Place wrapped prawns, noodle-end side down, in single layer on tray. Cover; refrigerate 30 minutes.

Cut carrots, bell peppers and onions into long, thin strips.

Just before serving, heat vegetable oil in large pan; deep-fry prawns, in batches, until prawns are cooked through; drain on paper towels.

Heat butter and peanut oil in wok or large pan; stir-fry extra garlic, carrot, pepper, onion, sprouts and extra sauce until vegetables are just tender. Serve prawns on bed of stir-fried vegetables.

SERVES 4 TO 6

Prawns best marinated 1 day ahead

Storage Covered, in refrigerator

Opposite Fresh salmon, caper and dill frittata
Right Shanghaied prawns and stir-fried vegetables

Ca'noodling with vegetables

The profusion of exotic and exciting newcomers on the greengrocer's shelves has given us a new appreciation of vegetables. Toss with one of the startling variety of noodles now easily found at the supermarket, add a dash of inspiration from Asia and the Mediterranean, and you'll find there are whole new avenues to be explored. Creative cooks will reap rewards when they take a fresh look at the veggie patch.

GRILLED HALOUMI, TOMATO AND ARUGULA HOKKIEN MEE

Very today, this amalgam of Mediterranean flavors is tossed in the melting pot with one of the best-loved of all Asian noodles.

14 large (2²/₃lb) plum tomatoes, halved lengthwise
1¹/₂ tablespoons olive oil
2 teaspoons balsamic vinegar
¹/₂ teaspoon salt
1 teaspoon cracked black pepper
1 bulb garlic, unpeeled
2 teaspoons balsamic vinegar, extra
¹/₂ cup vegetable stock
1¹/₄lb Hokkien mee
12oz haloumi or fontina cheese
8oz arugula, trimmed

Place tomatoes, cut-side up, on wire rack over baking dish; drizzle with combined oil and vinegar, sprinkle with combined salt and pepper. Wrap garlic in foil; place on rack with tomatoes.

Bake tomatoes, uncovered, and garlic at 350°F for 1 hour. Cover tomatoes with foil, bake 30 minutes. When garlic is cool enough to handle, peel; reserve pulp.

Blend or process half the tomatoes with garlic pulp, extra vinegar and stock until pureed.

Meanwhile, rinse noodles under hot water; drain. Transfer to large bowl; separate noodles with fork. Cut haloumi or fontina into ¹/₄-inch slices; cook on heated oiled griddle until cheese is browned lightly.

Just before serving, gently toss noodles in large bowl with pureed tomato mixture, remaining tomato halves, cheese slices and torn arugula.

SERVES 4

Best made just before serving

EGGPLANT TIMBALES WITH ROASTED TOMATO SAUCE

Because of its supple texture once it's cooked, somen works particularly well as the major ingredient in the timbale filling. If you have to substitute it, use a similarly fine, dried thin wheat noodle.

1 large eggplant
coarse cooking salt
4oz somen
1½ tablespoons olive oil
1 medium leek, sliced thinly
1 medium carrot, grated coarsely
1 medium zucchini, grated coarsely
4 eggs, beaten

1½ tablespoons chopped
  fresh oregano
¼ cup cream
½ cup crumbled feta cheese
¼ cup coarsely grated
  parmesan cheese

ROASTED TOMATO SAUCE
3 (1lb) small tomatoes, halved
1 teaspoon salt
2 cloves garlic, crushed
¼ cup olive oil
½ teaspoon sugar
1 tablespoon red wine vinegar

Slice eggplant thinly, place on wire rack, sprinkle with salt; let stand 30 minutes. Rinse under cold water; pat dry with paper towels. Cook eggplant on heated oiled griddle (or grill or barbecue) until browned lightly both sides.

Meanwhile, cook noodles in large pan of boiling salted water, uncovered, until just tender; drain. Heat oil in medium pan; cook leek, carrot and zucchini, stirring, until vegetables are soft. Transfer to large bowl; stir in noodles, eggs, oregano, cream and cheeses.

Overlap 4 eggplant slices over base and side of each of four 1¼-cup ovenproof dishes, extending eggplant slices slightly above edge of dishes. Divide noodle mixture among prepared dishes; fold eggplant over filling. Top timbales with remaining eggplant slices, pressing down firmly.

Cover timbales with foil, place on oven tray; bake at 350°F about 35 minutes or until firm. Serve timbales with Roasted Tomato Sauce.

Roasted Tomato Sauce Place tomatoes in baking dish, sprinkle with salt and combined garlic and 1¹/₂ tablespoons of the oil. Bake, uncovered, at 450°F about 20 minutes or until soft; cool. Blend or process tomatoes, remaining oil, sugar and vinegar until pureed. Press through fine sieve into small pan, discard skins; stir over medium heat until hot.

SERVES 4

Eggplant timbales best made just before serving. Roasted tomato sauce can be made 1 day ahead

Storage Covered, in refrigerator

Opposite Eggplant timbales with roasted tomato sauce
Above Mixed-mushroom ragout with baked ricotta

MIXED-MUSHROOM RAGOUT WITH BAKED RICOTTA

Chinese wheat noodles which have had a small amount of dehydrated egg powder used in their manufacture add just the right amount of color to this delicate recipe.

1lb ricotta cheese
2 egg yolks
3 cloves garlic, crushed
¹/₄ cup chopped fresh chives
¹/₄ cup dry white wine
2 tablespoons butter
7oz brown mushrooms, sliced finely
5oz oyster mushrooms, sliced finely
4oz enoki mushrooms
6oz dried yolk noodles

Oil deep 8-inch square cake pan; line base and sides with baking paper.

Combine cheese, yolks, 2 cloves of the garlic and 3 tablespoons of the chives in medium bowl; spread into prepared pan, smooth top. Cover pan with foil; place in baking dish with enough boiling water to come halfway up sides of pan. Bake at 350°F about 1 hour or until firm; remove foil, bake about 10 minutes or until browned lightly. Remove from oven; remove pan from dish, allow to cool.

Boil wine in large pan until reduced by half. Add butter, remaining garlic and mushrooms; cook, stirring, until mushrooms are soft. Add remaining chives.

Meanwhile, cook noodles in large pan of boiling salted water, uncovered, until just tender; drain. Rinse under hot water; drain. Cover to keep warm.

Cut baked ricotta into 8 triangles; divide triangles among 4 serving plates. Place equal parts of noodles and mushroom mixture on triangles.

SERVES 4

Noodles and mushroom ragout best made just before serving. Baked ricotta can be made 1 day ahead

Storage Covered, in refrigerator

GOAT CHEESE AND ROAST VEGETABLE TERRINE

The sheet of fresh rice noodle used here, unfolded, looks like a big, white tea-towel. Use soon after buying them because the older they are, the more likely these noodles are to break; keep refrigerated.

1 large eggplant
2 medium yellow zucchini
4 medium sweet red bell peppers
8oz spinach, trimmed
8oz mild firm goat cheese
1 egg, beaten
8oz piece fresh rice noodle

LEMON MAYONNAISE
1 egg yolk
3 teaspoons Dijon mustard
1/2 teaspoon salt
2 teaspoons lemon juice
1/2 cup light olive oil
1/2 teaspoon cracked black pepper
1/2 teaspoon grated lemon rind
3 tablespoons lemon juice, extra

Cut eggplant and zucchini lengthwise into 1/4-inch slices. Place, in single layer, on oven trays; coat with cooking oil spray, grill until browned lightly.

Quarter peppers; remove seeds and membranes. Roast under broiler or in 500°F oven, skin-side up, until skin blisters and blackens. Wrap pepper pieces in plastic or paper for 5 minutes; peel.

Boil, steam or microwave spinach until tender; drain. Chop half the spinach roughly; combine with cheese and egg in large bowl.

Oil 6 x 10-inch loaf pan, line base with parchment, extending paper over 2 long sides. Cut a 8 x 16-inch rectangle from noodle sheet; place in prepared pan, extending over 2 long sides. Top with the remaining spinach, half of the pepper, cheese mixture, zucchini, remaining half of the pepper, then the eggplant. Fold noodle sheets over eggplant; cover pan tightly with foil.

Bake at 325°F for 1 hour. Cool terrine 15 minutes before turning onto plate. Serve terrine, cut into slices, with Lemon Mayonnaise.

Lemon Mayonnaise Blend or process egg yolk, mustard, salt and juice until smooth. With motor operating, gradually pour in oil; process until thick. Stir in pepper, rind and extra juice.

SERVES 4 TO 6

Both terrine and mayonnaise can be prepared 1 day ahead

Storage Covered, separately, in refrigerator

ROAST WINTER VEGETABLES WITH SPLIT PEA SAUCE

We used a simple Chinese flat dried wheat noodle that was gutsy enough to be able to hold its own against the robust quality of the combined vegetables.

1¹/₂lb pumpkin, chopped
1 medium rutabaga, chopped
2 medium parsnips, chopped
2 large carrots, chopped
1 large onion, sliced
6 cloves garlic, peeled
¹/₄ cup olive oil
1¹/₂ tablespoons sumac [see Glossary] or tamarind
10oz dried wheat noodles
3 tablespoons chopped fresh cilantro

SPLIT PEA SAUCE
¹/₂ cup yellow split peas
3 cups vegetable stock
1 small onion, chopped finely
2 cloves garlic, crushed
1 teaspoon ground cumin
1 teaspoon ground coriander
1¹/₂ tablespoons lemon juice
¹/₄ cup water

Brush vegetables with combined oil and sumac or tamarind; place, in single layer, in large baking dish. Bake, uncovered, at 450°F about 30 minutes or until vegetables are browned and just tender.

Meanwhile, cook noodles in large pan of boiling salted water, uncovered, until just tender; drain. Cover to keep warm.

Combine vegetables in large bowl with noodles and coriander. Serve with hot Split Pea Sauce.

Split Pea Sauce Rinse peas under cold water; drain. Combine peas, 2 cups of the stock, onion and garlic in a large pan. Bring to boil; simmer, uncovered, about 30 minutes or until peas are soft. Blend or process pea mixture with spices and combined remaining stock, juice and water until pureed. Return to pan; stir over heat until hot.

SERVES 6

Vegetables and noodles best prepared just before serving. Split pea sauce can be made 1 day ahead

Storage Covered, in refrigerator

Opposite Goat cheese and roast vegetable terrine
Below Roast winter vegetables with split pea sauce

◱ **DRIED EGG NOODLES** are sometimes labeled tamago ramen, ba mee or dahn mein, and come in various thicknesses and colors from the addition of artificial or vegetable dyes. Some Asian dried egg noodles are very similar to their Italian cousins fettuccine and tagliatelle. In some recipes, fresh egg noodles can be used instead of dried if they are soaked (rather than boiled) in hot water just until tender. With all noodle ingredients, feel free to use one for the other, bearing in mind the necessary differences in cooking times and methods.

FAVA BEAN, GARBANZO AND LEMON THYME WITH NOODLES

The pulses make this dish seem Middle-Eastern in origin but the addition of lemon thyme and aged parmesan makes it a unique dish that succeeds on its own merits.

2/3 cup dried garbanzos
1/3 cup olive oil
1 large onion, chopped
3 medium sweet red bell peppers, seeded, chopped
2 cloves garlic, crushed
3 medium tomatoes, peeled, seeded, chopped
1 cup vegetable stock
1 teaspoon sugar
1lb frozen fava beans, cooked, peeled
2 1/2 tablespoons chopped fresh lemon thyme
1/3 cup finely grated parmesan cheese
8oz dried egg noodles
1/2 cup grated parmesan cheese, shaved

Cover garbanzos with cold water in medium bowl; let stand, covered, overnight.

Drain garbanzos then cook, uncovered, in medium pan of boiling salted water until just tender; drain.

Meanwhile, heat oil in large pan; cook onion, peppers and garlic, stirring, 15 minutes. Add tomato; cook, stirring, 10 minutes. Add stock, sugar and garbanzos; cook, covered, 5 minutes. Add fava beans, thyme and grated cheese; stir until hot.

Meanwhile, cook noodles in large pan of boiling salted water, uncovered, until just tender; drain. Gently toss noodles in large bowl with bean mixture; top with parmesan cheese.

SERVES 4

Best made just before serving

Above Fava bean, garbanzo and lemon thyme with noodles
Right Beet-tinted noodles with white beans

BEET-TINTED NOODLES WITH WHITE BEANS

Similar in appearance to a fine tagliolini, the dried Chinese flat wheat noodle used in this recipe was porous enough to absorb the beet color extremely well.

1 cup dried cannellini or
    navy beans
2 medium uncooked beets, grated
12oz dried wheat noodles
3 tablespoons vegetable oil
5 cloves garlic, crushed
3 tablespoons coarsely grated
    lemon rind
12 fresh water chestnuts, chopped

¹/₂ cup olive oil
¹/₄ cup balsamic vinegar
¹/₄ cup lemon juice
3 tablespoons chopped fresh chives
2 teaspoons sugar

Cover beans with cold water in medium bowl; let stand, covered, overnight.

Drain beans, then cook, uncovered, in medium pan of boiling salted water until just tender; drain.

Bring 6 cups of salted water to boil in large pan; simmer beets, uncovered, 5 minutes. Add noodles to pan; return to boil then remove from heat immediately. Let stand, stirring occasionally, until noodles are just tender and have absorbed beet color. Drain; cover to keep warm.

Heat oil in wok or large pan; stir-fry beans, garlic, rind and water chestnuts, until water chestnuts are just tender and browned lightly. Stir in combined remaining ingredients; cook, stirring, until hot. Divide noodles among serving plates; top with water chestnut mixture.

SERVES 4 TO 6

Best made just before serving

MEXI-VEGGIES WITH TOASTED TORTILLA CHIPS

This "South of the Border" combination of ingredients makes a wonderfully satisfying main course for a Saturday night supper.

1¹/₂ tablespoons olive oil
1 medium onion, sliced
2 teaspoons ground cumin
2 teaspoons ground coriander
3 small orange sweet
   potatoes, chopped
1 medium sweet red bell
   pepper, chopped
1 medium yellow bell
   pepper, chopped
2 corn cobs, chopped
15oz can meatless chili
15oz can tomatoes
1 cup vegetable stock
6 10-inch flour tortillas
4oz dried rice noodles
1 cup coarsely grated
   cheddar cheese

GUACAMOLE
2 small avocados
¹/₃ cup sour cream
1¹/₂ tablespoons lemon juice
1 medium tomato, peeled,
   seeded, chopped
1 small red onion, chopped finely
3 tablespoons chopped
   fresh cilantro

Heat oil in large pan; cook onion, stirring, until soft. Add cumin and coriander; cook, stirring, 1 minute. Stir in sweet potato, peppers, corn, beans, undrained crushed tomatoes and stock. Bring to boil; simmer, uncovered, about 10 minutes.

Cut each tortilla into 6 wedge-shaped pieces, place on oven tray in single layer; toast in 350°F oven about 5 minutes or until crisp and browned lightly.

Meanwhile, place noodles in large heatproof bowl, cover with boiling water, let stand until just tender; drain. Rinse under cold water; drain.

Gently stir noodles into vegetable mixture; divide mixture among 6 flame-proof serving dishes. Sprinkle with cheese; broil until cheese melts.

Serve Mexi-Veggies accompanied with tortilla chips and Guacamole.

Guacamole Blend or process avocados, sour cream and juice until just smooth; place in medium serving bowl, stir in tomato, onion and cilantro.

SERVES 6

Best made just before serving

Above Mexi-veggies with toasted tortilla chips
Opposite Creamy spinach and ricotta pancake torte

CREAMY SPINACH AND RICOTTA PANCAKE TORTE

Fresh egg noodles form part of the batter for this luscious stack of pancakes sandwiched with a creamy cheese, toasted pine nut and fresh spinach filling.

2lb spinach, trimmed
1¼lb ricotta cheese
⅓ cup pine nuts, toasted
3 tablespoons cream
7oz fresh egg noodles
¾ cup all-purpose flour
3 eggs, beaten
1 cup milk

TOMATO AND SWEET RED
BELL PEPPER SAUCE
2 medium sweet red bell peppers
2 cloves garlic, unpeeled
¼ cup olive oil
1 large onion, chopped
2 15oz cans tomatoes
¼ cup firmly packed chopped
**   fresh basil**

Boil, steam or microwave spinach until just wilted; drain. Rinse under cold water; drain. Squeeze as much liquid as possible from spinach; chop finely. Combine spinach with cheese, nuts and cream in large bowl.

Cook noodles in large pan of boiling salted water, uncovered, until just tender; drain. Rinse under cold water; drain. Chop noodles coarsely.

Sift flour into large bowl; gradually stir in combined eggs and milk, beat until smooth. Stir in noodles. Pour a quarter of the noodle mixture into large heated oiled pan, spread to 8-inch circle; cook until browned lightly both sides. Repeat with remaining mixture.

Place 1 pancake into deep 8-inch-round cake pan, spread over a third of the spinach mixture; top with another pancake. Repeat layering with remaining pancakes and spinach mixture, finishing with a pancake.

Bake, covered, at 350°F for about 30 minutes or until hot. Cut into wedges, serve with warmed Tomato and Sweet Red Bell Pepper Sauce.

Tomato and Sweet Red Bell Pepper Sauce Quarter peppers; remove and discard seeds and membranes. Roast pepper and garlic with 3 tablespoons of the oil in small baking dish, uncovered, at 400°F for 30 minutes. Remove from pan. Cover pepper with plastic or paper; let stand 5 minutes, peel away skin. Squeeze pulp from unpeeled garlic into small bowl.

Meanwhile, heat remaining oil in pan; cook onion, stirring, until soft. Add undrained crushed tomatoes, bring to boil; simmer, uncovered, 5 minutes. Blend or process tomato mixture with pepper, garlic pulp and basil until almost smooth.

SERVES 6

Best made just before serving. Tomato and Sweet Red Bell Pepper sauce can be made 1 day ahead

Storage Covered, in refrigerator

NOODLE PRIMAVERA

Our variation of the Italian classic sauce is so good you'll want to use it all the time – whether or not you use the fresh egg noodles shown here or the more traditional dried fettuccine.

1¹/₂ tablespoons olive oil
1 medium onion, sliced
1 clove garlic, crushed
1lb asparagus, trimmed, cut into
 1¹/₂-inch pieces
2 cups frozen peas
1²/₃ cups creme fraiche
¹/₄ cup vegetable stock
3 tablespoons Dijon mustard
¹/₃ cup coarsely grated
 parmesan cheese
¹/₄ cup chopped fresh mint
12oz fresh egg noodles

Heat oil in large pan; cook onion and garlic, stirring, until onion is soft. Add asparagus; cook, stirring, about 1 minute or until almost tender. Add peas and combined creme fraiche, stock and mustard; cook, over medium heat, stirring, about 5 minutes or until thickened slightly. Stir in cheese and mint.

Meanwhile, cook noodles in large pan of boiling salted water, uncovered, until just tender; drain. Gently toss noodles in large bowl with asparagus mixture.

SERVES 4 TO 6

Best made just before serving

Above Noodle primavera
Above right Eggplant, tomato and bocconcini towers
Right Tofu and vegetable curry

squash. Bring to boil; simmer, covered, until squash is almost tender. Add beans and pepper; simmer until beans are just tender. Add tofu; stir until hot.

Meanwhile, cook noodles in large pan of boiling salted water, uncovered, until just tender; drain. Divide noodles among serving bowls; top with vegetable curry.

SERVES 6

Best made just before serving

EGGPLANT, TOMATO AND BOCCONCINI TOWERS

Substitute rice vermicelli, if you prefer, for the bean thread noodles we used, and mozzarella if bocconcini is unavailable.

2¹/₂ oz bean thread noodles
¹/₃ cup vegetable oil
2 small eggplants
3 medium plum tomatoes, sliced
¹/₄ cup balsamic vinegar
¹/₄ cup olive oil
3oz bocconcini or mozzarella cheese

PESTO
1 cup firmly packed fresh basil
¹/₂ cup coarsely grated parmesan cheese
2 cloves garlic
1¹/₂ tablespoons olive oil
1¹/₂ tablespoons pine nuts, toasted
¹/₄ cup buttermilk

Place noodles in medium heatproof bowl, cover with boiling water, let stand until just tender; drain. Pat dry with paper towels. Heat vegetable oil in small pan; fry ³/₄ oz bundles of noodles, in batches, until just browned. Drain bundles on paper towels; you need 12 bundles.

Cut each eggplant into 6 slices; place on wire rack. Sprinkle eggplant slices with salt; let stand 30 minutes. Rinse eggplant thoroughly under cold water; pat dry with paper towels.

Place eggplant and tomato slices on oiled oven tray; brush with combined vinegar and olive oil. Grill eggplant, both sides, until browned lightly.

Cut cheese into ¹/₄-inch slices. Top 6 of the noodle bundles with a slice of eggplant, tomato, cheese and some of the Pesto. Repeat layering, ending with cheese and a drizzle of Pesto.

Pesto Blend or process all ingredients until pureed.

SERVES 6

Pesto can be made 1 day ahead

Storage Covered, in refrigerator

TOFU AND VEGETABLE CURRY

We used fresh egg noodles but use whatever you like, since the noodle here merely replaces the rice usually eaten with a curry.

3 tablespoons peanut oil
2 large onions, sliced
¹/₄ cup curry powder
1¹/₂ cups coconut milk powder
3 cups warm water
4 bay leaves
1 cinnamon stick
1¹/₄lb butternut squash, peeled, cut into 1-inch pieces
1lb green beans, trimmed, halved
1 medium sweet red bell pepper, chopped
7oz firm fresh tofu, drained, chopped
7oz fresh egg noodles

Heat oil in large pan; cook onions, stirring, until soft. Add curry powder; cook, stirring, about 1 minute or until fragrant. Add blended coconut milk powder and water, bay leaves, cinnamon stick and

QUARTET OF BEANS
IN A CHILI LIME SAUCE

Arrowroot noodles are notable more for their interesting texture than their flavor. Substitute bean thread noodles if you wish.

9oz arrowroot noodles
8oz frozen fava beans,
    thawed, peeled
5oz green beans, sliced
5oz long beans, sliced
5oz butter beans, sliced
vegetable oil, for deep-frying
1/4 cup capers, drained
1 1/2 tablespoons olive oil
6 cloves garlic, crushed
1 small red onion, chopped
4 small fresh red chilis, seeded
3 tablespoons finely grated lime rind
1/2 cup vegetable stock
2/3 cup cream
12 black olives, seeded, sliced

Cook noodles in large pan of boiling salted water, uncovered, until just tender; drain. Rinse under cold water; drain.

Boil, steam or microwave beans, separately, until just tender; drain. Heat vegetable oil in small pan; deep-fry capers until crisp. Drain on paper towels.

Heat olive oil in wok or large pan; stir-fry garlic, onion, chili and rind until onion is soft. Add stock, cream, olives, beans and noodles; cook, stirring gently, until sauce thickens and mixture is hot.

SERVES 4

Best made just before serving

Below Quartet of beans in a chili lime sauce
Opposite Tempura on rice-sticks with beet chips

TEMPURA ON RICE-STICKS
WITH BEET CHIPS

Any noodle can be used here, but deep-fried rice sticks harmonize nicely with the crunch of the tempura and beets.

vegetable oil, for deep-frying
4oz dried rice noodles
2 large uncooked beets
2 egg yolks
2 cups iced water
1 1/3 cups all-purpose flour
5oz firm tofu, cubed
3 1/2 oz snow peas, trimmed
8oz asparagus, trimmed, sliced
1 large green zucchini, sliced
2 medium yellow zucchini, sliced
3 1/2 oz green beans, sliced
1 large red onion, sliced
2 cups cauliflower, chopped
rice flour
1/4 cup mirin
1/2 cup light soy sauce
1 1/2 tablespoons sugar
1 1/2 tablespoons sweet chili sauce

Heat vegetable oil in large pan; deep-fry noodles, in batches, until puffed. Drain noodles on paper towels.

Using a vegetable peeler, slice beets into paper-thin strips. Reheat same oil; deep-fry beet, in batches, until crisp. Drain on paper towels.

Just before serving, combine egg yolks and water in medium bowl; stir in sifted flour all at once. Do not overmix; mixture should be lumpy.

Reheat vegetable oil in same pan. Toss tofu and all vegetables in rice flour; shake off excess. Dip tofu and vegetables, 1 at a time, in batter. Deep-fry tofu and vegetables until browned lightly; drain on paper towels. Divide noodles among serving plates; top with tempura tofu and vegetables. Serve with sauce made with combined remaining ingredients and crisp beet chips.

SERVES 4

Best made just before serving

☐ **ARROWROOT NOODLES** are semi-transparent, off-white noodles made, not surprisingly, from starch extracted from arrowroot tubers. They are a favored ingredient in the spicy cuisine of the western Chinese province of Szechuan, and in Korea, a cold-climate country where these noodles are featured in hearty soups.

ROASTED TOMATOES
WITH SAUCY BASIL NOODLES

Fresh egg noodles are the perfect foil for this rich sauce and luscious tomatoes.

12 (1³/₄lb) medium plum tomatoes
1 teaspoon salt
**1 teaspoon freshly cracked
    black pepper**
1 teaspoon sugar
2 cups firmly packed fresh basil
1 clove garlic, peeled
**¹/₄ cup coarsely grated
    parmesan cheese**
¹/₃ cup olive oil
1¹/₂ tablespoons balsamic vinegar
3oz prosciutto, sliced finely
12oz fresh egg noodles
¹/₃ cup pine nuts, toasted

Halve tomatoes; place, cut-side up, on wire rack in baking dish. Sprinkle with combined salt, pepper and sugar; bake in 400°F oven about 30 minutes or until soft.

Blend or process basil, garlic, cheese, oil and vinegar until almost pureed.

Place prosciutto, in single layer, on oven tray; grill until crisp, turning once during cooking.

Meanwhile, cook noodles in large pan of boiling salted water, uncovered, until just tender; drain.

Gently toss basil mixture in large bowl with noodles; divide among serving plates. Top with tomato halves and prosciutto; sprinkle with pine nuts.

SERVES 4 TO 6

Best made just before serving

GLOSSARY

chorizo sausage

black olives

kalamata olives

BANANA LEAVES can be ordered from fruit and vegetable stores. Usually 1 leaf is cut into about 10 pieces. Cut with a sharp knife close to the main stem then immerse in hot water so that leaves will be pliable.

BEAN CURD see **Tofu**.

BLACK BEANS are salted, fermented and dried soy beans. Soak, drain and rinse dried beans; chop before, or mash during, cooking to release flavor. **Black bean sauce** is made from fermented soy beans, spices, water and wheat flour.

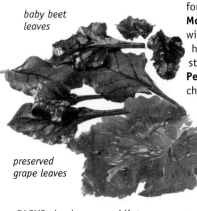

baby beet leaves

preserved grape leaves

BLINI also known as blintzes or crepes. Buckwheat pancakes originally from Russia where they were eaten with caviar. Their fillings can be sweet for desserts, or savory for finger foods.

BONITO FLAKES a dried fish from the mackerel family, available both in flaked form and as an ingredient in the Japanese stock, dashi.

BREADCRUMBS
1- or 2-day-old bread made into crumbs by grating, blending or processing.

BUTTERMILK low-fat milk cultured to give it a slightly sour, tangy taste; low-fat yogurt can be substituted.

CHEESE
Bocconcini small rounds of fresh "baby" mozzarella, traditionally made in Italy from buffalo milk. Spoils rapidly so must be refrigerated, in brine, for a maximum of 2 days.
Cheddar use an aged, hard, strong-flavored variety.
Feta Greek in origin; a crumbly goat or sheep milk cheese having a pronounced sharp, salty taste.
Goat made from goat milk, has an earthy, strong taste; comes in both soft and firm textures.
Haloumi a firm, cream-colored sheep milk cheese matured in brine; somewhat like a minty, salty feta in flavor. Good grilled. Substitute with fontina if unavailable.
Mozzarella a semi-soft cheese with a delicate, fresh taste; has a low melting point and stringy texture when heated.
Pecorino hard, dry, yellow cheese, which has a sharp, pungent taste. Originally from sheep milk, now made with cow milk. If unavailable, use parmesan.
Ricotta a sweet, fairly moist, fresh-curd cheese with a fairly low fat content.
Romano a hard, straw-colored cheese with a grainy texture and sharp, tangy flavor; usually made from a combination of cow and goat or sheep milk. A good cheese for grating.
Smoked cheddar a hard cheddar cheese which has been placed, un-cut, in a smoke room for about 6 hours. There is also artificially smoked cheese where flavor is added to the milk before the cheese is made.

CHEESECLOTH plain loosely woven cotton fabric. Often used to strain stocks and sauces. Paper coffee filters may be substituted.

CHERMOULLA spicy Moroccan mixture of fresh and ground spices including coriander, cumin and paprika. This paste may be covered with a thin layer of oil to preserve it.

CHILI SAUCE
Hot we used a hot Chinese variety made from bird's-eye chilis, salt and vinegar. Use sparingly, increasing the quantity to your taste.
Sweet a comparatively mild, Thai-type commercial sauce made from red chilis, sugar, garlic and vinegar.

CHINESE BARBECUED PORK also known as chow shu. Traditionally cooked in special ovens, this pork has a sweet-sticky coating made from soy sauce, sherry, five-spice and hoisin sauce. It is available from Asian food stores. To make Chinese barbecued pork, charcoal grill strips of pork butt (about 3lb) after marinating overnight in 2 tablespoons hoisin sauce, $1/4$ cup each catsup and sugar, 1 teaspoon salt, and 1 table-spoon soy sauce. Unused portions may be wrapped and frozen for future use.

CHOY SUM flowering bok choy or white cabbage; similar to chinese broccoli.

blue mussels

CILANTRO also known as coriander leaves or chinese parsley; a green pungent herb used in Asian and Latin American cooking.

COCONUT
Milk pure, unsweetened coconut milk available in cans.
Milk powder coconut milk that has been dehydrated and ground to a fine powder.

CREAM
Fresh (minimum fat content 30-36%) also known as light or heavy whipping cream.
Sour (minimum fat content at least 18%) a thick, commercially cultured soured cream.

CREME FRAICHE a fresh matured cream that has been commercially lightly soured; available in cartons from delicatessens and supermarkets. To make creme fraiche, combine $1 1/4$ cups cream with $1 1/4$ cups sour cream in bowl; cover, let stand at room temperature until mixture thickens. This will take 1 or 2 days, depending on room temperature; refrigerate once fermented. This makes about $2 1/2$ cups.

clams

large white scallops

ground turmeric

fresh turmeric

tamarind

sweet Spanish paprika

hot paprika

baby capers

regular capers

ground cumin

cumin seeds

CURRY

Madras paste consists of coriander, cumin, pepper, turmeric, chili, garlic, ginger, vinegar and oil.
Powder a blend of ground spices used for convenience when making Indian food.

Can consist of some of the following spices in varying proportions: dried chili, cinnamon, coriander, cumin, fennel, fenugreek, mace, cardamom and turmeric. Choose mild or hot to suit your taste and the recipe.
Red paste consisting of chili, onion, garlic, oil, lemon rind, shrimp paste, cumin, paprika, turmeric and pepper.

DASHI the basic fish and seaweed stock that accounts for the distinctive flavor of many Japanese dishes. It is made from dried bonito flakes and kelp (kombu). Instant dashi powder, also known as dashi-no-moto, is available from Asian speciality stores.

FISH

Barramundi large fish found in coastal rivers of northern Australia and the Pacific. It has a firm, white flesh with a large flake and mild flavor. Available whole, as steaks, cutlets or fillets. If unavailable, use perch.
Cod an excellent eating fish with white, firm flesh. When cooked, it is moist with a large flake. Usually available as skinless fillets.

FISH SAUCE also called nam pla or nuoc nam; made from pulverized, salted, fermented fish, most often anchovies. Has a pungent smell and strong taste. There are many different fish sauces on the market, and the intensity of flavor varies with each one.

FLOUR

All-purpose flour made from wheat.
Rice a very fine flour, made from ground white rice.

GARAM MASALA a blend of spices, originating in North India; based on varying proportions of cardamom, cinnamon, cloves, coriander, fennel and cumin, roasted and ground together.

GARBANZOS also known as chickpeas; an irregularly round, sandy-colored legume.

GHERKIN sometimes known as a cornichon; young, dark-green cucumbers grown especially for pickling.

HOISIN SAUCE a thick, sweet and spicy Chinese paste made from salted fermented soy beans, onions and garlic; used as a marinade or baste, or to accent stir-fries and barbecued or roasted foods.

ITALIAN PARSLEY flat-leaf parsley; more pungent that curled leaf variety.

KAFFIR LIME LEAVES available frozen or dried in Asian markets; used for seasoning; leaves are from South Africa and Asia.

KETJAP MANIS Indonesian sweet, thick soy sauce which has sugar and spices added. If your grocer is unable to order this ingredient for you, substitute thick teriyaki sauce.

MASALA blended spices which are whole, powdered or paste; can include herbs and other ingredients.

MIRIN a sweet white wine made from rice. Available at Japanese food shops and some grocery stores.

MISO is grouped into 2 main categories – red and white, although the "red" is dark brown in color and "white" is more the color of weak tea.

baby bok choy

arugula

Made in Japan, miso is a paste made from cooked, mashed, salted and fermented soy beans, and it is a common ingredient in soups, sauces and dressings.

MUSTARD

Dijon a distinctively sharp French mustard.
Stone ground a coarse-grain; made of crushed mustard seeds and Dijon-style mustard.

NORI a type of dried seaweed used in Japanese cooking as a seasoning, garnish or for sushi. Sold in thin sheets.

OIL

Hazelnut a mono-unsaturated oil, made in France, extracted from crushed hazelnuts.
Olive a mono-unsaturated oil, made from the pressing of tree-ripened olives; especially good for everyday cooking and in salad dressings. Light describes the mild flavor, not the fat level.

canned green peppercorns

Szechuan peppercorn

black peppercorns

star anise

napa or Chinese cabbage

spinach

baby spinach leaves

choy sum

Peanut pressed from ground peanuts; most commonly used oil in Asian cooking because of its high smoke point.
Sesame made from roasted, crushed, white sesame seeds; a flavoring rather than a cooking medium.

OYSTER SAUCE Asian in origin, rich, brown sauce made from oysters, brine, salt and soy sauce then thickened.

PITA Lebanese bread or pocket bread; a Middle Eastern, wheat-flour bread, usually sold pre-packaged in large, flat pieces easily separated into two paper-thin rounds. Comes in smaller, thicker pieces commonly called **Pocket Pita**.

PLUM SAUCE a thick, sweet and sour dipping sauce made from plums, vinegar, sugar, chilies and spices.

POUSSIN a young chicken weighing no more than 1lb; if unavailable, Cornish game hen may be substituted.

PROSCIUTTO salted-cured, air-dried (unsmoked), pressed ham or lamb; usually sold in paper-thin slices, ready to eat.

PUFF PASTRY SHEETS frozen sheets of puff pastry made from wheat flour; vegetable margarine or butter, salt, food acid and water.

RICE
Calrose is a medium grain rice that is extremely versatile; can substitute for short- or long-grain rice if necessary.

RICE PAPER mostly from Vietnam (banh trang). Made from rice paste and stamped into rounds with a woven pattern. Stores well at room temperature, although they are quite brittle and will break if dropped.

cilantro roots

fresh and dried kaffir lime leaves

dried bay leaves

Dipped momentarily in water they become pliable wrappers for fried food and for eating fresh (uncooked) vegetables.

ROSTI small patties or cakes.

SAMBAL OELEK (also ulek or olek) Indonesian in origin; a salty paste made from ground chilies.

SAMBOL OR SAMBAL thick spicy sauce, originating in India, made with vinegar or lime juice, chilis, onions and other ingredients.

SAMOSA small crescent-shaped deep-fried pastries filled with combinations of meat, vegetables and other ingredients.

SCORE shallow cuts, usually in a criss-cross pattern, over meat, vegetables or seafood. Often used on squid.

SEASONED PEPPER a packaged preparation of combined black pepper, sweet red bell pepper and paprika.

SHRIMP PASTE also known as trasi or blanchan; it is a strong-scented, almost solid, preserved paste made of salted dried shrimp. Used as a pungent flavoring in many Southeast Asian soups and sauces.

SNOW PEAS bright green flat, edible pod peas used often in Asian cooking; sugar snaps, also edible pod peas may be substituted.

SOY SAUCE made from fermented soy beans. Several variations are available in most supermarkets.
Dark used for color as well as flavor, particularly in North Chinese cooking.
Light a soy sauce with one third of the salt removed.

SPRING ROLL WRAPPERS are also sometimes called egg roll wrappers; they come in various sizes and can be purchased fresh or frozen from Asian supermarkets. Made from a delicate wheat-based pastry, they can be used for making gow gee and samosas as well as spring rolls.

SHIRATAKE transparent thin noodles, sold both dried and fresh, made from a Japanese root vegetable called konnyaku.

STRINGHOPPERS a Sri Lankan indigenous noodle about the size of a saucer made by forcing rice-flour batter through a perforated mold. Available in Indian or Asian markets.

SUGAR we used granulated sugar, also known as crystal sugar, unless otherwise specified.
Brown a soft, fine, granulated sugar containing molasses to give its characteristic color.
Raw a naturally golden brown, granulated sugar.

SUMAC a purple-red and astringent spice ground from the berries of shrubs that flourish wild around the Mediterranean (do **NOT** confuse with common name for Poison Ivy); adds a tart, lemony flavour. Can be found in Middle Eastern markets. Tamarind can be substituted.

TAMARIND CONCENTRATE a thick, purple-black, ready-to-use paste extracted from the pulp of the tamarind bean; used as is, with no soaking, stirred into sauces, dressings and casseroles.

shiitake

shimeji

button

Swiss brown

enoki

oyster

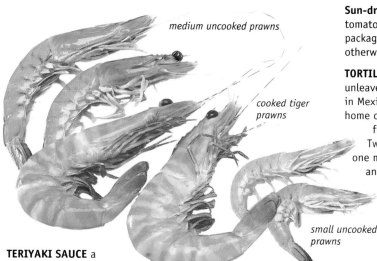

medium uncooked prawns

cooked tiger prawns

small uncooked prawns

Sun-dried (dehydrated tomatoes) sun-dried tomatoes packaged in oil, unless otherwise specified.

TORTILLA thin, round, unleavened bread originating in Mexico; can be made at home or purchased frozen, fresh or vacuum-packed. Two kinds are available, one made from wheat flour and the other from corn.

UDON Japanese wheat flour noodle.

Red wine based on fermented red wine.
Rice made from fermented rice, colorless and flavored with sugar and salt. Also sometimes called seasoned rice vinegar.
White made from spirit of cane sugar.
White wine made from fermented white wine.

WASABI an Asian horseradish used to make a fiery sauce traditionally served with Japanese raw fish dishes. Sold as paste in tubes or as powder in 1oz cans.

plain nori

toasted nori

TERIYAKI SAUCE a homemade or commercially bottled sauce usually made from soy sauce, mirin, sugar, ginger and other spices; it imparts a distinctive glaze when brushed on grilled meat.

TOFU also known as bean curd, an off-white, custard-like product made from the "milk" of crushed soy beans; comes fresh as soft or firm, and processed as fried or pressed dried sheets. Leftover fresh tofu can be refrigerated, in water (which is changed daily), for up to 4 days. Silken tofu refers to the method it's made by, strained through silk, rather than its texture.

Bean curd pouches pockets of fried bean curd (tofu) which are able to be opened out to take a filling. Available from Asian food stores.

TOMATO
Pear, yellow a relatively recent addition to specialty markets, this tiny pear-shaped tomato is less than 1-inch long.
Paste a concentrated tomato puree used for flavoring.
Puree canned pureed tomatoes. Substitute with fresh peeled and pureed tomatoes.
Plum egg-shaped tomato used fresh or to make sauces and pastes: also known as roma or plum.

fresh water chestnuts

inarizushi bean curd pouches

canned water chestnuts

VINEGAR
Balsamic
authentic only from the province of Modena, Italy; made from a regional wine of white Trebbiano grapes specially processed then aged in antique wooden casks to give it its uniquely exquisite,pungent flavor.

Cider made from fermented apples.

Raspberry made from fresh raspberries steeped in a white wine vinegar.

WATER CHESTNUTS resemble chestnuts in appearance, hence the English name. They are small brown tubers with a crisp, white, nutty-tasting flesh. Their crunchy texture is best experienced fresh, however, canned water chestnuts are more easily obtained and can be kept about a month, once opened, under refrigeration.

WONTON WRAPPERS fresh pastry sheets made with egg; substitute spring roll wrappers.

sesame seeds

polenta

black mustard seeds

red lentils

yellow split peas

INDEX

Anchovy dressing, 37
Arrowroot noodles, 110
Avocado sushi, salmon and, 20

Baked beef 'n' noodles, 61
Baked ricotta, mixed-mushroom
  ragout with, 101
Baked trout with orange
  hazelnut glaze, 85
Banana leaves, cajun-style
  fish wrapped in, 94
Barbecued octopus with
  stringhoppers, 88
Baskets, sweet-sour beef
  in noodle, 56
Bean, garbanzo and lemon thyme
  with noodles, fava, 104
Bean-curd pouches with wasabi,
  gingery fried, 18
Bean soup, roasted tomato
  and pinto, 7
Bean-thread crunch, lion
  heads with, 18
Bean thread noodles, 9, 21
Beans, beet-tinted
  noodles with white, 105
Beans in a chili lime sauce,
  quartet of, 110
Beef
  'n' noodles, baked, 61
  and lime noodles, curried, 63
  in noodle baskets,
    sweet-sour, 56
  noodle soup, Vietnamese, 10
  noodles, satay, 51
  salad, sesame, 36
  soup, hearty Szechuan, 13
  stringhopper salad, 37
  stroganoff with a trio
    of mushrooms, 53
  sukiyaki, 47
  with somen, teriyaki, 55
  with sun-dried tomato sauce, 42
  ramen and bok choy stir-fry, 52
Beet chips, tempura on
  rice-sticks with, 110
Beet-tinted noodles with
  white beans, 105
Birthday noodles, 79
Black-bean sauce, sea
  scallops in, 19
Blini, Siberian salmon with soba, 91
Brete's chicken curry, 70
Broth with garlic croutons,
  meatballs in, 7

Cajun-style fish wrapped in
  banana leaves, 94
Char kway teow, 81
Char-grilled chili squid with
  ribbon vegetables, 39
Chermoulla, noodle and prawn, 94
Chicken
  char kway teow, 81
  combination chow mein, 67
  and noodles in
    radicchio bowls, 76
  curry, Brete's, 70
  fattoush with soba, 72
  fillets with soba and arugula, 68
  lime-roasted spring chicken
    with noodles, 66
  lion heads with bean-thread
    crunch, 18

mee krob, 76
noodle soup, 13
patties with lime sauce, chili, 25
salad, hazelnut, 36
samosas with peanut
  sambal, noodly, 24
soup, coconut, 9
spinach lasagna, 78
with garlic mashed potatoes,
  rice stick-crusted, 70
with mixed green
  vegetables, sesame, 74
with noodles, red pesto, 75
chilled soba with fennel and, 64
cucumber and sprout salad, 32
larb-style, 80
mushroom and vermicelli
  risotto, 73
Penang stir-fry noodles
  and caramelized, 68
Spanish chili, 79
Squash and sweet potato stew, 71
Chilled noodles, Japanese, 26
Chilled soba with fennel
  and chicken, 64
Chili chicken patties with
  lime sauce, 25
Chili cucumber sauce, 26
Chili squid packages, Oriental, 95
Chinese roast pork with stacked
  noodle omelettes, 48
Chops with thyme-toasted
  noodles, lamb, 50
Chow mein, combination, 67
Cilantro pesto, crusty lamb chops
  with, 59
Coco-chili prawns on a
  noodle nest, 93
Coconut chicken soup, 9
Coconut masala, south Indian grilled
  fish with, 89
Coconut spinach soup, 4
Coleslaw with fried
  noodles, crunchy, 39
Combination chow mein, 67
Crab and smoked salmon springtime
  salad, fresh, 40
Crab, goat cheese and chive rosti, 87
Creamy lime noodles with
  smoked salmon, 86
Creamy spinach and ricotta
  pancake torte, 107
Crisp prawns, 22
Crispy noodle triangles, 57
Crunchy coleslaw with
  fried noodles, 39
Crunchy noodle pizzas, 78
Crusty lamb chops with
  cilantro pesto, 59
Curried beef and lime noodles, 63
Curry, Brete's chicken, 70
Curry, tofu and vegetable, 109

Dipping sauce, 26
Dolmades, lamb, 29
Dried egg noodles, 104
Dried rice noodles, 76
Dried wheat noodles, 68
Duck salad, Peking, 41
Dumplings with plum sauce,
  steamed pork, 28

Eggplant timbales with roasted
  tomato sauce, 100

Eggplant, tomato and
  bocconcini towers, 109

Fattoush with soba, chicken, 72
Fava bean, garbanzo and lemon
  thyme with noodles, 104
Feta and sweet red pepper salad, 34
Fish with coconut masala, south
  Indian grilled, 89
Fish wrapped in banana leaves,
  Cajun-style, 94
Fresh crab and smoked salmon
  springtime salad, 40
Fresh rice noodle sheets, 92
Fresh rice noodles, 13
Fresh salmon, caper and dill
  frittata, 96
Fresh wheat noodles, 61
Fritters, vegetable and ramen, 24

Garbanzo and lemon thyme with
  noodles, broad bean, 104
Garlic dressing, 56
Garlic mashed potatoes, rice
  stick-crusted chicken with, 70
Garlic mayonnaise, 45
Gingery fried bean-curd pouches
  with wasabi, 18
Goat cheese and chive rosti, crab, 87
Goat cheese and roast
  vegetable terrine, 102
Grape leaves filled with lamb
  (lamb dolmades), 29
Green peppercorn dressing, 68
Grilled haloumi, tomato and arugula
  Hokkien mee, 98
Grilled vegetable and
  haloumi stacks, 35
Guacamole, 107

Haloumi, tomato and arugula
  Hokkien mee, grilled, 98
Hazelnut chicken salad, 36
Hearty Szechuan beef soup, 13
Hokkien mee, 57
Hokkien mee, grilled haloumi,
  tomato and arugula, 98
Hot and sour seafood soup, 12

Japanese chilled noodles, 26

Kofta, pork and veal, 44

Laksa paste, 11
Laksa, prawn, 11
Lamb
  and lentil soup, Moroccan, 14
  and spinach salad, 34
  chops with cilantro pesto,
    crusty, 59
  chops with thyme-toasted
    noodles, 50
  dolmades, 29
  roasted tomatoes and walnuts, 47
  shanks with baked noodles, 61
  stir-fried udon and crispy, 62
  with crispy noodle triangles,
    orange ginger, 57
  with garlic noodles, 45
Larb-style chicken, 80
Lasagna, chicken spinach, 78
Lemon-marinated tuna salad, 32
Lemon mayonnaise, 102
Lemon soy dressing, 84
Lentil soup, Moroccan lamb and, 14

Lime and wasabi seafood noodles, 82
Lime chili sauce, 22
Lime dressing, 33
Lime, tomato and scallop salad, 33
Lime-roasted spring chicken
  with noodles, 66
Lion heads with bean-thread
  crunch, 18
Long and short soup, 15

Madras, veal and green bean, 55
Malaysian fried noodles (char
  kway teow), 81
Masala, south Indian grilled fish
  with coconut, 89
Mayonnaise, garlic, 45
Meatballs in broth with garlic
  croutons, 7
Mee goreng, 59
Mee, Hokkien, 57
Mee krob, 76
Mexi-veggies with toasted
  tortilla chips, 106
Mini spring rolls with chili
  cucumber sauce, 26
Miso soup, 9
Mixed seafood in a
  pumpkin basket, 86
Mixed-mushroom ragout with
  baked ricotta, 101
Moroccan lamb and lentil soup, 14
Mushroom ragout with baked ricotta,
  mixed-, 101
Mushrooms, beef stroganoff
  with a trio of, 53
Mustard-curry pork slices in
  mushroom sauce, 45

Noodle(s)
  and prawn chermoulla, 94
  arrowroot, 110
  baskets 56
  bean thread, 9, 21
  birthday, 79
  bundles, 22
  crispy, 59
  crispy triangles, 57
  dried egg, 104
  dried rice, 76
  dried wheat, 68
  eating, 50
  fresh rice, 13, 92
  fresh wheat, 61
  identity crises, 94
  Japanese chilled, 26
  nest, coco-chili prawns on a, 93
  pancakes, red curry, 22
  Peking, 29
  pizza, crunchy, 78
  primavera, 108
  ramen, 25
  rice stick, 33
  Singapore, 48
  Shanghai, 7
  sheets, fresh rice, 92
  shirataki, 47
  soba, 73, 85
  somen, 55
  storage, 35.
  stringhoppers, 89, 115
  substituting, 38, 41, 44
  triangles, crispy, 57
  udon, 63
  zaru-soba, 26

Noodly chicken samosas with peanut sambal, 24
Nori, 21

Octopus with stringhoppers, barbecued, 88
Omelettes, Chinese roast pork with stacked noodle, 48
Orange ginger lamb with crispy noodle triangles, 57
Orange hazelnut glaze, baked trout with, 85
Oriental chili squid packages, 95

Pancake torte, creamy spinach and ricotta, 107
Pancakes, red curry noodle, 22
Patties with lime sauce, chili chicken, 25
Peanut chili sauce, 22
Peanut sambal, 24
Peking duck salad, 41
Peking noodles, 29
Penang stir-fry noodles and caramelized chicken, 68
Pepper, sweet red, salad feta and, 34
Pepper, sweet red, sauce, roasted, 19
Peppers, sweet red, filled with pork and veal, roast, 52
Pesto, 78
Pesto chicken with noodles, red, 75
Pesto, crusty lamb chops with cilantro, 59
Phad Thai, 88
Pho bo (Vietnamese beef noodle soup), 10
Pinto bean soup, roasted tomato and, 7
Pizzas, crunchy noodle, 78
Polenta batons, Szechuan prawns with noodle, 90
Polenta-peppered tuna with rice noodle ribbons, 92
Pork
    and veal kofta, 44
    and veal, roast sweet red bell peppers filled with, 52
    dumplings with plum sauce, steamed, 28
    Hokkien mee, 57
    mee goreng, 59
    sang choy bow revisited, 21
    slices in mushroom sauce, mustard-curry, 45
    with stacked noodle omelettes, Chinese roast, 48
Poussin, 66
Prawn(s)
    and stir-fried vegetables, Shanghaied, 97
    char kway teow, 81
    chermoulla, noodle and, 94
    combination chow mein, 67
    crisp, 22
    hot and sour seafood soup, 12
    laksa, 11
    long and short soup, 15
    on a noodle nest, coco-chili, 93
    pad Thai, 88
    salad, sweet chili, 38
    tempura, soba with, 84
    with noodle polenta batons, Szechuan, 90
Primavera, noodle 108
Pumpkin basket, mixed seafood in a, 86
Pumpkin soup, Thai, 8

Quartet of beans in a chili lime sauce, 110

Radicchio bowls, chicken and noodles in, 76
Ragout with baked ricotta, mixed-mushroom, 101
Ramen, 25
Red curry noodle pancakes, 22
Red pesto chicken with noodles, 75
Rice noodle ribbons, polenta-peppered tuna with, 92
Rice stick noodles, 33
Rice-paper rolls, Vietnamese, 16
Rice stick-crusted chicken with garlic mashed potatoes, 70
Risotto, chicken, mushroom and vermicelli, 73
Roast sweet red bell pepper sauce, 18
Roast sweet red bell pepper filled with pork and veal, 52
Roast vegetable terrine, goat cheese and, 102
Roast winter vegetables with split pea sauce, 103
Roasted tomato and pinto bean soup, 7
Roasted tomato sauce, 100
Roasted tomatoes and walnuts, lamb with, 47
Roasted tomatoes with saucy basil noodles, 112
Rolls, Vietnamese rice-paper, 16
Rosti, crab, goat cheese, and chive, 87

Salad
    char-grilled chili squid with ribbon vegetables, 39
    chicken, cucumber and sprout, 32
    coleslaw with fried noodles, crunchy, 39
    feta and sweet red bell pepper, 34
    fresh crab and smoked salmon springtime, 40
    grilled vegetable and haloumi stacks, 35
    hazelnut chicken, 36
    lamb and spinach, 34
    lemon-marinated tuna, 32
    lime, tomato and scallop, 33
    Peking duck, 41
    sesame beef, 36
    smoked salmon, avocado and udon, 30
    stringhopper, 37
    sweet chili prawn, 38
Salmon and avocado sushi, 20
Salmon with soba blini, Siberian, 91
Salmon, avocado and udon salad, smoked, 30
Salmon, caper and dill frittata, fresh, 96
Salmon, creamy lime noodles with smoked, 86
Samosas with peanut sambal, noodly chicken, 24
Sang choy bow revisited, 21
Satay beef noodles, 51
Sauce
    black bean, 48
    chermoulla, 94
    chili cucumber, 26
    dipping, 26
    guacamole, 106
    lime chili, 22
    peanut chili, 22
    peanut sambal, 24
    roast sweet red bell pepper, 18
    roasted tomato, 100
    split pea, 103
    tomato, 29

tomato and sweet red bell peppers, 107
Saucy basil noodles, roasted tomatoes with, 112
Scallop salad, lime, tomato and, 33
Sea scallops in black-bean sauce, 19
Seafood in a pumpkin basket, mixed, 86
Seafood noodles, lime and wasabi, 82
Seafood soup, hot and sour, 12
Sesame beef salad, 36
Sesame chicken with mixed green vegetables, 74
Shanghai noodles, 7
Shanghaied prawns and stir-fried vegetables, 97
Shanks with baked noodles, lamb, 61
Shirataki, 47, 115
Short soup, long and, 15
Siberian salmon with soba blini, 91
Singapore noodles, 48
Smoked salmon springtime salad, fresh crab and, 40
Smoked salmon, avocado and udon, 30
Smoked salmon, creamy lime noodles with, 86
Soba, 73, 85
Soba and arugula, boneless chicken breasts, 68
Soba blini, Siberian salmon with, 91
Soba with fennel and chicken, chilled, 64
Soba with prawn tempura, 84
Soba, chicken fattoush with, 72
Soba, zaru-, 26
Somen, 55
Soup
    chicken noodle, 13
    coconut chicken, 9
    coconut spinach, 4
    hearty Szechuan beef, 13
    hot and sour seafood, 12
    long and short, 15
    meatballs in broth with garlic croutons, 7
    miso, 9
    Moroccan lamb and lentil, 14
    roasted tomato and pinto bean, 7
    Thai pumpkin, 8
    Vietnamese beef noodle, 10
South Indian grilled fish with coconut masala, 89
Spanish chili chicken, 79
Spinach and ricotta pancake torte, creamy, 107
Spinach lasagna, chicken, 78
Spinach salad, lamb and, 34
Spinach soup, coconut, 4
Split pea sauce, 103
Spring Chicken with Noodles, lime-roasted, 66
Spring rolls with chili cucumber sauce, mini, 26
Squid packages, Oriental chili, 95
Squid with ribbon vegetables, char-grilled chili, 39
Steamed pork dumplings with plum, 28
Stew, chicken, pumpkin and sweet potato, 71
Stir-fried udon and crispy lamb, 62
Stir-fry noodles and caramelized chicken, Penang, 68
Stir-fry, beef, ramen and bok choy, 52
Stroganoff with a trio of mushrooms, beef, 53
Stringhopper salad, 37
Stringhoppers, 89, 115
Stringhoppers, barbecued octopus with, 88

Stroganoff with a trio of mushrooms, beef, 53
Sukiyaki, 47
Sun-dried tomato sauce, beef with, 42
Sushi, salmon and avocado, 20
Sweet chili prawn salad, 38
Sweet red pepper salad, feta and, 34
Sweet red pepper filled with pork and veal roast, 52
Sweet-sour beef in noodle baskets, 56
Szechuan beef soup, hearty, 13
Szechuan prawns with noodle polenta batons, 90

Tempura on rice-sticks with beet chips, 110
Tempura, soba with prawn, 84
Teriyaki beef with somen, 55
Terrine, goat cheese and roast vegetable, 102
Thai pumpkin soup, 8
Thyme-toasted noodles, lamb chops with, 50
Timbales with roasted tomato sauce, eggplant, 100
Tofu and vegetable curry, 109
Tomato and bocconcini towers, eggplant, 109
Tomato and pinto bean soup, roasted, 7
Tomato sauce, 29
Tomatoes with saucy basil noodles, roasted, 112
Tortilla chips, Mexi-veggies with toasted, 106
Towers, eggplant, tomato and bocconcini, 109
Trout with orange hazelnut glaze, baked, 85
Tuna salad, lemon-marinated, 32
Tuna with rice noodle ribbons, polenta-peppered, 92

Udon, 63
Udon and crispy lamb, stir-fried, 62

Veal and green bean Madras, 55
Veal kofta, pork and, 44
Veal, roasted sweet red bell peppers filled with pork and, 52
Vegetable and haloumi stacks, grilled, 35
Vegetable and ramen fritters, 24
Vegetable curry, tofu and, 109
Vegetable terrine, goat cheese and roast, 102
Vegetables with split pea sauce, roast winter, 103
Veggies with toasted tortilla chips, Mexi-, 106
Vietnamese beef noodle soup, 10
Vietnamese rice-paper rolls, 16

White beans, beet-tinted noodles with, 105
Wontons, 15

Zaru-soba, 26

Can't boil an egg?

Sweet Potato Leek and Sage Frittata (*Healthy Eating Vegetarian*, page 28)

...Then bake it.